GOD'S LOVE AND GOD'S CHILDREN

Expository Readings in Epistle to Romans

GOD'S LOVE

AND

GOD'S CHILDREN

A Study of Romans VIII. 14 to XVI. 27

A COMPANION VOLUME TO
" *God's Gospel and God's Righteousness* " (*Chapters I. to V.*) and
" *God's Gift and Our Response* " (*Chapters V. to VIII*)

By

PHILIP MAURO

ATTORNEY AT LAW
Author of "The Number of Man," "Life in the Word," etc.

WIPF & STOCK · Eugene, Oregon

Wipf and Stock Publishers
199 W 8th Ave, Suite 3
Eugene, OR 97401

God's Love and God's Children
A Study of Romans VIII. 14 to XVI. 27
By Mauro, Philip
ISBN 13: 978-1-62032-528-5
Publication date 8/15/2012
Previously published by Flemming H. Revell Co., 1914

Preface

This volume is a sequel to two books on the earlier chapters of Romans, taking up the subject of that Epistle at Chapter 8, verse 14. The titles of the two preceding books are respectively, " God's Gospel and God's Righteousness," and " God's Gift and Our Response."

The quotations of Scripture in this volume are generally from the Authorized Version. But in some cases we have departed from that excellent version for the sake of greater clearness, and have adopted the literal rendering of " The Englishman's Greek New Testament," Bagster & Sons, London.

Contents

8 Contents

CHAPTER I

Sons of God

" For as many as are led by the Spirit of God, they
are the SONS OF GOD." (Rom. 8:14.)

At *Rom. 8: 14,* quoted above, the progress of the teaching of this Epistle brings us to a new subject,—" Sons
of God." It is the first time this subject is mentioned
in the Epistles, in the order in which they occur in the
New Testament. At verse 13 we take leave of the subject of *sin and death,* which has been at the forefront
of the apostolic teaching from Chap. 5:12, where it is
introduced. From that section of the Epistle (5:12–
8:13) we learn the deeply solemn and important truth
that sin, which entered the world through Adam, and
was followed by death, its inevitable consequence, holds
absolute dominion over all men. We learn also that
the *law,* which was given by God to His people Israel,
afforded no means of escape from the dominion of sin
and death; for the law brought no aid to man, but, on
the contrary, it required something *from* man. It
demanded obedience to the holy and righteous requirements of God. Thus the effect of the law was to prove
that man, in the state of nature, is wholly incapable of
meeting God's just requirements.

It should be always borne in mind that the law of
Moses required of man only what man *ought* to do.
It was not a system of harsh and burdensome demands,

9

but, on the contrary, was just and right. Moreover it was (as the Israelites fully understood) for their good. As Moses said, "And the Lord commanded us to do all these statutes, to fear the Lord our God, *for our good always*" (Deut. 6:24).

But man, in the state to which sin had brought him, had not the power to do even what his own intelligence showed him he ought to do, in his own interest. The experience of Saul of Tarsus as a man under law was the experience of every conscientious Israelite who set himself in his own will, to keep the requirements of the law. This is his testimony: "To WILL is present with me; but how to WORK OUT that which is good I find not. For the good that I WILLED I practice not; but the evil which I WILLED NOT, that I do" (Rom. 7:19, 20). And this would be the experience of every man when subjected to the same test. Hence the law tested and revealed the condition of all mankind. It showed that human "flesh," which God had created in innocence, had become through the "one offence" of Adam, the "flesh of sin" (8:3), that is to say, sin's possession and property.

The law, then, served to reveal on the one hand, the incapacity of human beings to meet the righteous requirements of God, and to reveal, on the other hand, the presence in man, and the mighty power and exceeding sinfulness, of SIN. "For by the law is the knowledge of sin." "Nay," says one who had been under the law, "I had not known sin, but by (means of) the law." "But sin, that it might appear sin"—that is, might be manifested in its real character—"working *death* in me by (means of) that which is good (the law); that sin by the commandment might become exceedingly sinful " (3:20; 7:7, 13). Thus, while " the sting of death is sin," it appears that " the strength of sin is the law "; although the law itself is " holy." (1 Cor. 15:56; Rom. 7:12).

The law, then, afforded no way of escape for man from the dominion of sin. But Jesus Christ, the incarnate Son of God, sent forth by His Father in the likeness of flesh of sin, endured sin's penalty on behalf of the ungodly, in order to put away sin by the sacrifice of Himself. " Christ died *for the ungodly.*" " While we were yet *sinners,* Christ died for us." " For in that He died, He died unto *sin* once for all."

And not only did He die to sin, thus annulling the power of death over those for whom He died; but He also *rose again.* And, being raised from the dead He dieth no more; death hath *no more dominion* over Him.

Thus a new sphere of human existence is brought to light in a Man, who was dead, and Whom God raised up from among the dead. This is the sphere of " eternal life in Christ Jesus our Lord." In that sphere, grace reigns through righteousness; whereas in the sphere of the man who disobeyed God,—the first Adam,— sin reigned unto death (5:21).

The Gospel proclaims this new sphere of human life in Christ (in contrast with the dying condition of those who are in Adam). For the purpose and grace of God are now made manifest by the appearing of our Saviour, Jesus Christ, " Who hath abolished (annulled) *death* and brought *life* and incorruptibility to light *through the Gospel* " (2 Tim. 1:10).

Those who obey the Gospel, whether Jews or Gentiles, are delivered from the dominion of sin and death, being turned from the authority of Satan (who has the power of death) unto God (Acts, 26:18). They are delivered from the authority of darkness, and are translated into the Kingdom of the Son of God's love (Col. 1:12). They thus belong to an entirely new sphere; they are under the authority that rules in that sphere; and they are entitled to all the benefits pertaining to it, among which benefits are "righteousness, peace, and joy in the Holy Ghost" (Rom. 14:17).

It is revealed, however, that the corrupted flesh ("flesh of sin") remains in those who have been reconciled to God by the death of His Son; and it is further revealed that the mind of the flesh is not subject to God's law, and indeed cannot be (8:7). The "flesh" is *always* subject to "the law of sin." (7:25.)

Hence there is need not only of deliverance from the *dominion* of sin and death, but also of deliverance from "the *law* of sin and death." This deliverance the apostle Paul knew as a personal experience; and he declares that it came "through Jesus Christ our Lord" (7:25), by the instrumentality of "the LAW of THE SPIRIT OF LIFE IN CHRIST JESUS." (8:2.)

Thus, while we must face the solemn fact that the "flesh" in the justified man is no more subject to God's authority than the flesh in an unconverted person, nevertheless we have also the encouraging revelation that, in the sphere where grace reigns, there is provision whereby we (believers) may have practical deliverance from the *law* (or control) of sin. For though the flesh is in us, we are not debtors to the flesh to live according to its inclinations (or "mind"). That is to say, we are not under obligation or compulsion to live after the manner of those who "are (have their existence) in the flesh." There is another "law" to which we may, if we will, be in subjection, namely "the law of the Spirit of life in Christ Jesus."

In considering this matter of the believers' life in the mortal body we come upon one of the strongest statements in all the Scripture concerning our responsibility. For it is plainly stated that if we live after the flesh,— seeing there is no obligation so to do,—we shall die. But, on the other hand, if we, THROUGH THE SPIRIT, do put to death the doings of the body, it is promised that we shall live. (8:13.) Then follows the verse quoted at the head of our chapter. " For as many as are led by the Spirit of God, they are the sons of God."

We see, then, that the subject of " sons of God" is introduced in connection with the subject of the presence and ministry on earth of the SPIRIT OF GOD. We believe it to be important to notice this, and are persuaded that valuable instruction may be obtained thereby.

Previous portions of the Epistle speak of what THE FATHER has done. He has justified freely by His grace all who believe on His Son. He has set forth His Son for a Mercy-seat through faith. He has raised up Jesus our Lord from the dead.

Other passages speak of what has been accomplished by THE SON. Through Him we have peace with God, and through Him we have access into this sphere of grace in which we stand. We were reconciled to God by the death of His Son. We also joy (or boast) in God, through our Lord Jesus Christ, by Whom we have now received the reconciliation.

And now we come to a section of the Epistle which speaks of the work of the SPIRIT OF GOD, who is on earth during the present dispensation, and it is as a sub-topic in this section that we find teaching in regard to the sons of God. The appropriateness of this is apparent when we recall that those who are the children of God are born of the Spirit.

The Epistle to the Romans, however, does not contain an explanation of who the children of God are. That explanation is found in other Scriptures. Our text does not say that all children of God are led by the Spirit of God, or that one is not a child of God unless he is led by the Spirit of God. On the contrary, the context plainly implies that some children of God are *not* in subjection to the law of the spirit of life in Christ, being not led by the Spirit. The statement is that as many as *are* led by the Spirit, they are the sons of God; and the implication is that it is the privilege of every child of God to be under the guidance of the Holy Spirit. Submission to God, however, must be voluntary. "Let not sin reign in your mortal bodies that ye should obey it in the lusts thereof. Neither yield ye your members as instruments of unrighteousness unto sin. But yield yourselves unto God, and your members instruments of righteousness unto God." "I beseech you therefore, brethren, by the mercies of God, that ye present your bodies, a living sacrifice, holy, acceptable unto God." All these and other passages show that the children of God are called upon to act willingly in accordance with the position that God's grace has given them.

The law of the Spirit is the law of life; but it is also the "law of liberty," and by it we shall be judged (James 2:12). The state of "sons" is a state of liberty. They may walk after the Spirit, or they may walk after the flesh.

It follows from what has been said, that we should

trace our present subject " sons of God " from the passage where the Holy Spirit is first mentioned. This is in Chap. 5, ver. 5, where we find the words, " because the love of God is shed abroad in our hearts by the Holy Ghost which is given unto us."

CHAPTER II.

The Love of God Poured out in our Hearts.

(Rom. 5:5; 8:14–16.)

It is surely a matter of much significance that the first mention of the Holy Spirit in Romans occurs in connection with the great theme of the Love of God. This fact, if rightly used, will be found to be the key to knowledge of the highest value. The knowledge of God is the highest of all knowledge; and to know God is to know Love; for God is love. " He that loveth not knoweth not God; for God is love." (1 John 4: 8).

The mention of the Holy Spirit also occurs in connection with the subject of the " Sons of God "; and this connection is also significant, for God's love has its manifestation in His children. Love cannot be except in relation to one who is loved; and the nearest and highest relation of the loved one to the one who loves is that of son. Hence the Son of God is " the Son of His love," and to Him He gives " the kingdom," that is the supreme honour, rule, authority and government (Col. 1:13).

In earlier portions of Romans mention is made of the Gospel of God, the Power of God, the Righteousness of God, the Forbearance of God, the Wrath of God, the Grace of God, and the Glory of God. 'But at Rom. 5:5 we reach the highest attribute of God—namely the

Love of God.   And it is there stated that the love of God
is shed abroad in our hearts by the Holy Spirit who is
given to us.

It will be greatly to our profit to look more closely
at the several statements contained in this verse.

The love of God is *shed abroad*.   The word here rendered "shed abroad" is used elsewhere in connection
with the sending of the Holy Spirit of God to men.   Thus,
the apostle Peter, citing the prophecy of Joel, said:
"And it shall come to pass in the last days, saith God,
that I will *pour out* of My Spirit upon all flesh . . .
and on My servants and on My handmaidens I will
POUR OUT in those days of My Spirit." (Acts 2:17–18.)
The word "pour out" is that rendered "shed abroad"
in Rom. 5:5.

And again, after having proclaimed the resurrection
of Jesus Christ, Peter said: "Therefore, being by the
right hand of God exalted, and having received of the
Father the promise of the Holy Ghost, He hath SHED
FORTH this, which ye now see, and hear " (Acts 2:33).

Thus, in Peter's address, as in Paul's Epistle (Rom.
5:5), the announcement of the POURING OUT of the Holy
Spirit follows immediately upon that of the resurrection of Jesus Christ from the dead.   The pouring out
of the Spirit is in fact the result of the resurrection of
Christ and His exaltation in heaven.

It is significant that the apostle Peter speaks of the
Holy Spirit as the " gift" and "promise" of "the
Father," although it was not given to him (Peter) at that
time to reveal that believers in Christ are brought into
the relation of sons to God the Father.   This word " the
Father," used by Peter on Pentecost, conveys to the
instructed saint the precious truth of the position given

to him in the "love of God." It also carries the mind
back to the last words of the Risen Lord prior to His
ascension, as recorded in the Gospel of Luke, "And
behold, I send the promise of MY FATHER upon you"
(Luke 24:49); and to those recorded in Acts. 1:4: " But
wait for the PROMISE OF THE FATHER, which ye have
heard of Me."

This "love of God" poured out in our hearts by the
Holy Spirit is contained by implication in the word
"Father." As another apostle declares it: "Behold,
what manner of *love* THE FATHER hath bestowed upon
us, that we should be CALLED THE SONS OF GOD." (1
John 3:1.) So we learn that the love of God poured
out in our hearts, is the knowledge conveyed there by
the Spirit of God of our relation of sons to the Father.
This is the practical outcome of " the great love wherewith He loved us even when we were dead in sins "
(Eph. 4:4). Nothing less would satisfy His heart or
adequately express His love for those for whom Christ
died. For "God commendeth HIS LOVE towards us in that
while we were YET SINNERS, Christ died for us." The
purpose thus to give eternal expression to His love towards
those whom He chose in Christ, was formed before the
foundation of the world. For we read in Eph. 1:4, 5,
"According as He hath chosen us in Him before the
foundation of the world, that we should be holy and
without blame before Him; IN LOVE having predestinated us unto the ADOPTION (place of sons) by Jesus
Christ unto Himself." (We agree with those who read
the words " in love " as belonging to ver. 5 and qualify-
ing " predestinated.")

God's love is poured out " in our hearts." The heart
is the region wherein the Spirit works the miracle of

regeneration. For it is written "And because ye are sons, God has sent forth the Spirit of His Son INTO YOUR HEARTS, crying Abba, Father " (Gal. 4:6).

This passage in Galatians throws light upon Rom. 5:5. By it we understand that the Spirit is sent forth by God into our hearts, making known the wondrous fact of relationship of children to the Father, enabling us to cry from the heart (not with the lips only) "Abba, Father." This action of the Spirit in our hearts enabling us to call God our " Father," is the outcome and expression of the love of God.

In full accord with this are the words of Rom. 8:16, "The Spirit Himself beareth witness with our spirit that we are the CHILDREN OF GOD."

" *The Holy Ghost who is given to us.*" The Spirit of God, in His manifold ministries is God's *gift*. Love ever shows itself in *giving* (John 3:16; Gal. 2:20). Again referring to the words of Peter on Pentecost we note his exhortation to "Repent and be baptized in the Name of Jesus Christ for the remission of sins, and ye shall receive the GIFT of the Holy Ghost " (Acts 2:38).

Likewise in Romans 5, justification from sins through Jesus Christ is followed by the *gift* of the Holy Spirit.

And again when Peter had preached to the Gentiles in the house of Cornelius, announcing the remission of sins, through the Risen Christ, to all who believe on Him, the Holy Spirit fell on all them which heard the word. Then those believers of the circumcision who came with Peter were astonished, "because that on the Gentiles also was POURED OUT the GIFT of the Holy Ghost " (Acts 10:43–45).

We learn then that the Holy Spirit is the "Gift" of the FATHER, promised by the Son, and bestowed on those

who believe. The Spirit is given in order to reveal to
their hearts the Father's love, which is expressed in
calling them into the relation of *sons* to Himself. This
promise of the Son of God on the eve of His departure
from the world is recorded five times in John's Gospel,
Chapters XIV–XVI. The following passage is specially pertinent:

" I will pray the Father, and He shall GIVE you another Comforter, that He may abide with you forever;
even the Spirit of truth; Whom the world cannot receive,
because it seeth Him not, neither knoweth Him; but
ye know Him; for He dwelleth with you and shall be
in you. I WILL NOT LEAVE YOU ORPHANS " (John 14:16–
18). This last promise, " I will not leave you orphans,"
has been fulfilled by the ministry of the Spirit of God,
witnessing to believers that they are the children of God.

CHAPTER III.

The Love of God and the Glory of God.

The relation of the last clause of Rom. 5:5 to the context is not easy to determine. The clause begins with the word "because." To which of the preceding statements does that word refer? Does hope make us not ashamed because the love of God is shed abroad in our hearts? There is seemingly no relation of cause and effect between these two statements, and the writer ventures to suggest that the word "because" connects with the end of verse 2. If this suggestion be correct the passage would read: "and (we) rejoice in hope of the glory of God, because the love of God is shed abroad in our hearts by the Holy Ghost Who is given to us." According to this reading verses 3 and 4, and the first clause of verse 5 form a parenthesis.

The sense appears to be as follows:

In the work of justifying the sinner from his sins there is no room at all for any man to "boast." Boasting is excluded (3:27). Abraham had nothing to boast of before God (4:2, the word rendered "glory" being the same word rendered "boast," in 3:27). Yet it is said in Chapter 5 that *after* we have been justified, we may boast (again we should read "boast" instead of "rejoice"); "we boast upon the hope of the glory of God." The reason why we boast upon this hope is that "the love of God has been shed abroad in our hearts by the Holy Spirit" assuring us that we are sons of God. God's gift of His Holy Spirit now imparts to us confidence to boast in the hope of His glory. Being the children of God, and being assured thereof by the witness of His Spirit, we have nothing to fear from the wrath to come at the appearing of the glory of God. That coming event is not now a matter of *fear* to us but of *hope*. The Spirit of God gives us the assurance of this; for we have not received the spirit of bondage again to fear (of coming wrath) but the Spirit of adoption, whereby we cry Abba, Father (8:15).*

That this is the purport of the Scripture we are studying is confirmed by those passages which refer to the Spirit of God given to God's children, as the "earnest" or "first fruits" of their future inheritance. (Rom. 8:15, 23; 2 Cor. 5:5; Eph. 1:11–14.) We shall not, at this point, examine those passages in detail. It will suffice to indicate that in the Scripture immediately before us, Rom. 8:14–30, the children of God are said to be "waiting for the adoption," (verse 23), and that, while awaiting the ADOPTION they have already received the SPIRIT of adoption (verse 15). It thus appears that the Spirit of God, given now to God's children, is directly related to that which is in store for them, namely, "the adoption." The characteristic effect of the Spirit of adoption upon our hearts is that He enables us to cry "Abba, Father." This cry expresses the *known relation of a son*, and the knowledge of that relation to God, imparted by His Spirit to our hearts, removes all fear as to the future purpose of God, enabling us rather to "boast"

* The term "adoption" requires explanation, which will be found in Chapter VI.

thereon. The love of the Father is perfect love, and "perfect love casteth out fear."

Verses 6–11 of Chapter 5 contain further reasons why believers, having been justified by the grace of God, can confidently hope for the glory that is to be revealed to us, the ground of that hope being firmly laid in the love of God.

God *commends* His love towards us as having this marvellous characteristic, namely, that it moved Him to give His own Son to die for us "while we were yet sinners," while we—that is to say, were yet everything that is abhorrent and repulsive to a Holy Being.

When a human being "loves" another, it is because of something attractive, seen or imagined, in that other. What men speak of as "love" is a sentiment *drawn out* of them by the attractions (real or fancied) of the beloved one. There is nothing specially to "commend" in such affection as this.

Divine love, which God here commends, is something radically different from the affection that is "natural" to the creature. It is not *drawn out* by any attraction in the object towards which it moves; but on the contrary, it proceeds towards that object by an irresistible power generated in the heart of God, a power so great as to overcome the repulsion which the corruption of the sinner must arouse in One Who is of purer eyes than to behold evil. The power to love *those who are the very reverse of what is lovable belongs to God alone.*

But there is more than this in the love towards us which God commends. Any act of loving-kindness, any mercy however small, done for "sinners," would be a wonderful display of love. But the love of God has gone to the length, inconceivable by us, of giving up His own Son to endure the shame and agony of death "for us," and this, " while we were yet sinners,"—that is, while we were fitting objects of detestation, and while we were in our hearts not lovers of God, but "enemies."

There are lengths and depths here which the finite being can never measure nor fathom. There is, in the first place, our own state as being "sinners." The *position* of the sinner with respect to God is *distance;* and his *state* is *corruption.* The distance from God of the sinner is immeasurable. We were indeed "afar off." Nor can we form any adequate conception of the hatefulness of our corrupted state as "sinners."

Then we think of the One whom the Father gave for our redemption. Who can estimate the value to the Father of His own and only Son?

Then we think of the awful experience to which the Son of God was delivered up on account of our offences. Who can fathom the depths of humiliation to which He descended when He became an offering for sin? Who can conceive His suffering when exposed to the Divine displeasure against sin? Who can know the feelings of the Father during that mysterious period when our redemption was being wrought out by His Holy One on the cross of shame?

God's love towards us which He commends is indeed too vast for our comprehension; and we cannot be thankful enough for any measure in which we have been enabled, by the work of His Spirit in our hearts, to know it. May the apostle's prayer be ever the expression of our own heart's desire, "That He would grant you, according to the riches of His glory to be strengthened with might *by His Spirit in the inner man*, that Christ may dwell in your hearts by faith; that ye, being rooted and grounded *in love,* may be able to comprehend with all saints, what is the breadth and length and depth and height; and TO KNOW THE LOVE OF CHRIST WHICH PASSETH KNOWLEDGE." (Eph. 3:16–19.)

This love of God toward us is made the foundation of an argument by which the apostle would fortify our hope of the coming glory. For, since God so manifested His love for us while we were "yet sinners" most assuredly we, "being now justified by His blood," shall be saved from wrath through Him. How different are we now, in God's sight, having been justified by His blood, every spot and stain removed, to what we were when "yet sinners"! "Much more" then, being now washed from our sins and cleansed from all unrighteousness by that which *alone* could cleanse the vile and guilty sinner, namely, the blood of Jesus Christ, God's Son, "we shall be saved from wrath through Him." "For if, when we were ENEMIES, we were reconciled to God by the DEATH of His Son, much more, BEING RECONCILED, we shall be saved by His LIFE." (5:9, 10.)

It is most desirable, for the comfort and assurance of our hearts, that we should realize the force of this argument, just as far as we have capacity to do so. There are two great contrasts presented in the verse last quoted. The first contrast has reference to the state of our own hearts towards God. When Christ died for us we were "enemies" of God. *Now* we have been "reconciled." If God would do a mighty work of love and power for us while we were at enmity with Him, "much more" will He do a lesser thing (save us out of the coming wrath) now that we have been reconciled to Him.

The second contrast has reference to the Son of God, comparing His *death,* with His *life.* That great and

unspeakable sacrifice, the *death* of the Son of God on
the cross, has been made. That sacrifice was a divine
necessity in order to accomplish the purpose of God,
and to secure the Father's object, which could only
be attained through blood-redemption. "The Son of
man *must be* lifted up." (John 3:14.) " Thus it *behooved*
the Christ to suffer and to rise from the dead the third
day " (Luke 24:46). "Christ *must needs* have suffered
and risen again from the dead " (Acts 17:3).

But there is now no need of any further sacrifice to
save the redeemed ones from the coming wrath of God.
In order to accomplish that, the Son of God needs not
again to *die* for us, but to *live* for us. He is able to save
to the uttermost them that come to God by Him, seeing
He *ever liveth* to make intercession for them (Heb.
7:25).

The ground of our hope then is unshakable. It is
in order that we might have a sure hope that these Scriptures are given to us. The possession of hope is one of
the essential characteristics of the children of God; and
the nature of hope is such that it belongs *only* to this
present time while we see not yet the things hoped for.
It is exceedingly important that we should all have
the Scriptural " hope," not only for our comfort and
peace, but that it may exert upon our hearts its intended
effect of purifying us from all desires for the things of
this present evil age.

Therefore we should pay earnest heed to the testimony
of the Scriptures that speak of the good things which
God has prepared for them that love Him, and which
He reveals to them by His Spirit. We shall then be
able to make our boast of the hope of the glory of God;
and not only so, but to boast in tribulation also, for we

shall know that tribulation worketh patience, and patience, experience; and experience, hope.

Tribulation is thus made to accomplish an important result; and, this being understood, we can boast in tribulation also. Its ultimate result is to impel us to lay hold upon the *hope* set before us. Hope is that which connects the heart with things yet future and "not seen." If things seen and present, that is to say, our circumstances in this world, are wholly to our liking, and our hearts are contented with them, there would be no place in us for hope. But if tribulation be our lot, then the hope of the glory that is to be revealed to us will have place in our hearts. For one who has peace with God through Jesus Christ, and a standing in the grace of God by Him, the product of tribulation is *patience*, that is to say, *endurance*. Tribulation, for such an one, worketh patience. And patience worketh experience, or proof. Thereby our faith is tested or proved, to make sure whether it be *real* faith; as was Abraham's faith, who "patiently endured" (literally *had long patience*); and as was the faith of Moses, who "*endured* as seeing Him Who is invisible." And the product of experience is *hope;* for they who stand the experience of enduring affliction have a real and ˙a firm hope, one that is sure and steadfast, and which "entereth into that within the veil,"—that is to say, connecting the heart with unseen things that are yet to be unveiled. For "if we hope for that we see not, then do we with patience wait for it." In Rom. 15:4 it is stated that the factors which produce hope are *patience* (endurance), and the *comfort* (or encouragement) *of the Scriptures*. As already stated, we need to be in a situation requiring an exercise of patience, in order that our hearts may turn with desire and expectation to things not seen as yet. But there would be no certainty or reality of good things to come but for the promises of the Word of God. Those promises constitute "the encouragement of the Scriptures," whereby hope is awakened in our hearts.

Thus it will be clearly seen that the hope of the glory awaiting the sons of God is firmly grounded upon the love of God; and that it is the Spirit of God Who now creates and sustains this hope in our hearts. "For we, THROUGH THE SPIRIT, wait for the HOPE of righteousness by faith " (Gal. 5:5).

CHAPTER IV.

Heirs of God.

(Rom. 8:17–22.)

The passage beginning Romans 8:14 contains an amplification of the first eleven verses of Chapter 5. Among the subjects found in those verses, and which are taken up for further discussion in Chapter 8, are the Holy Spirit, the Love of God, the Glory of God, Hope, Tribulation, and Patience.

The great subject of the Love of God spans and embraces this entire section of the Epistle. The section begins with the statement that God's love is shed abroad in our hearts by the Holy Spirit, and ends with the assurance that nothing, seen or unseen, present or future, shall be able to separate us from the love of God that is in Christ Jesus our Lord.

The broad divisions of the subject-matter of this portion of the book recall the promise of Psalm 84:11: "The Lord will give` grace and glory; no good thing will He withhold from them that walk uprightly;" (i.e., who walk not after the flesh but after the spirit). Accordingly we have first God's work of grace as set forth in the words: " Justified freely by His grace;" " It is of faith that it might be by grace, to the end the promise might be sure to all the seed;" "We have access by faith into this grace wherein we stand; " "The grace of God and the gift by grace hath abounded unto many; "

"Where sin abounded grace did much more abound;"
"Ye are not under law, but under grace."

But the " God of all grace" is also the "God of glory;"
and therefore, having received the grace, we may confidently hope for the glory. Chapters 6 and 7 of Romans
tell of deliverance from sin and death, and from the law,
through the *grace* of God; and Chapter 8 treats of
the *glory* of God.

The word "glory" is, when taken by itself, abstract
and vague. But by attention to the facts contained in
Rom. 8, we may form some definite ideas concerning
the glory which is to be manifested to us.

This coming "glory" includes all that the Father,
infinite in power and wealth, has planned to do for the
honour, joy, and blessedness of His children. Upon that
plan God had lavished the resources of His wisdom, power
and riches. It is His new creation in Christ Jesus. And
the central feature of that vast plan is the glory of His
own Son, Who glorified Him in the earth. For the great
object in view is "that He might be the Firstborn among
many brethren " (8:29).

The first consequence that results from sonship to
God is heirship. "If children, then heirs." This is
something we are able to comprehend, to some extent
at least. From our knowledge of the prospects of those
who are, by their natural birth, the children of persons
of great wealth and high worldly position, we can form an
idea of the prospects of the children of God.

God directs the special attention of His children to
their promised inheritance. That is therefore a fitting
subject for their contemplation. What God has planned
for them is surely worthy of their deepest interest. Not
that they should think of their inheritance apart from

the Lord; for it is in company with Himself that they shall possess and enjoy it. All things are given us "with Him." "How shall He not WITH HIM freely give us all things" (8:32). "God has spoken unto us in His Son, Whom He hath appointed Heir of all things" (Heb. 1:2, 3).

The verses that follow (19–25) tell us that the inheritance of God's children includes the material creation, the earth and all things upon, above, and beneath it.

But the "whole creation," when the children of God enter into possession of it, will be in a very different condition from that in which we now see it. Even now the earth and the things it produces are the objects of men's desires and efforts, and are well worthy of them. Men toil, and scheme, and suffer, and fight, and even die, in the attempt to gain possession of some part of the earth and its products. What will it be when the curse is removed? when every blighting influence, every destructive agency, every thing which wastes or corrupts or produces pain or sickness, or suffering or loss, is abolished? when the fruitfulness and beauty of the earth shall have been restored to their fulness? and when the glory of the Lord shall cover it, as the waters cover the sea? If we have heard with our ears and believed in our hearts God's revealed plans for His creation, which plans are to be consummated at "the manifestation of the sons of God," for which creation waits, we shall be more than content to walk as strangers and pilgrims in this present scene, and will accept with patience, and even with "boasting," whatever of suffering and trial may fall to us as our present portion.

Indeed there is a very pronounced encouragement given us to endure "the sufferings of this present time."

For it is evident that the measure of future glory will
bear a relation to that of the present sufferings. All
children are heirs. The fact of being a child makes one
an heir, without anything else. But all heirs will not
share alike, either as to the honour of their station, or
the extent of their possessions. Every Israelite had a
share in the inheritance; but there were very many
degrees of wealth and station. "One star differeth from
another star in glory. So also is the resurrection of the
dead."

In verse 17 there is an evident distinction drawn
between the children as a whole who are all heirs of God,
and those who suffer with Christ. These latter are
"joint-heirs" with Him. The construction of the sen-
tence shows clearly that the "joint-heirs" with Christ
are those who jointly suffer with Him now. In the
Greek there is a single word for "joint-heirs," and an
analogous word for "joint-sufferers." The parallel statements are these: "if children, then heirs, heirs indeed of
God"; "but joint-heirs with Christ if indeed we suffer
jointly with Him."

To be a joint-heir with Christ would carry with it a
share with Him in the rule and government of the creation, in other words, it would mean to reign with Him.
To the same effect it is written in 2 Tim. 2:11, 12: "It
is a faithful saying; for if we died with Him we shall
also live with Him; *if we suffer* we shall also *reign* with
Him." To "live with Him " is one thing. To "reign
with Him " is another thing.

His own promise is "To him that overcometh and
keepeth My works unto the end, to him will I give power
over the nations, and he shall rule them with a rod of
iron;" and again, "To him that overcometh will **I**

grant to sit with Me in My throne." (Rev. 2:26, 27; 3:21.)

In Rev. 20:4 it is said of those who were beheaded for the witness of Jesus and for the word of God, and which had not worshipped the beast, neither his image, neither had received his mark, that "they lived, and *reigned with Christ* a thousand years." They "lived" is one fact, and in addition to being raised into life, they also "reigned with Christ."

We know of no Scriptural support for the idea that all who are saved by the grace of God through faith will reign jointly with Christ. The foregoing Scriptures seem to refute that idea completely. All the children will share the inheritance—but not all will share the honours of the throne of Christ.

The verses which we now have under consideration direct our attention to the great contrast between the state in which God's children are now, and that in which they will be in the coming age; and also to the contrast between the state of creation as it now is, and as it will be in that age. The whole creation groans and travails in pain together up to the present moment. For creation was put in subjection to *vanity*, that is to say, has been made subject to the vain doings of men in their fallen state. This word "vanity" expresses God's judgment of all the great achievements upon which men pride themselves. All is vanity, and all is for that reason doomed to utter destruction. The man whom God endowed with the greatest portion of human wisdom said, "I have seen all the works that are done under the sun, and behold, ALL IS VANITY and vexation of spirit. . . . I made me great works, I builded me houses; I planted me vineyards," etc., giving a list of his great works, than which no man ever did greater; and when it was all done he says, " Then I looked on all the works that my hands had wrought, and on the labour that I had laboured to do: and behold, ALL WAS VANITY and vexation of spirit, and there was no profit under the sun " (Eccl. 1:14; 2:4–11).

Such is the present state of God's wonderful creation. It lies in the humiliating condition of subjection to man's doings, which, however much he may boast of them in his folly and ignorance, are all "vanity."

This subjection of the creation to vanity was "not willingly," or "by choice," but by reason of him who made it subject. The one who did this is generally taken to be Adam. But the words "who subjected it" imply an act of authority, and therefore it would seem that the reference is to the act of God, who laid upon the earth a curse for man's sake (Gen. 3:17, 18). The words "in sorrow (lit. *in pain*) shalt thou eat of it," have an echo in the words "travaileth together *in pain*." The words of Rom. 8:20, 21, namely, "in hope that the creation itself shall be delivered from the bondage of corruption into the liberty of the glory of the children of God," * also point to an act of God. Although God appointed for creation a period of sufferings, thus involving creation in the consequences of the sin of the man who was placed over it, He did so nevertheless "in hope" of a coming day of deliverence. None but God could place creation in subjection to vanity; and none but God could deliver it therefrom.

This verse (21) gives the contrast of the present state

---

* It is necessary to the understanding of this passage to note that the words " in hope " belong to the subject of verse 21, not to verse 20.

of creation "the bondage of corruption," with its future state "the liberty of the glory of the children of God." Creation has shared the bondage caused by the sin of Adam. It will also share the glorious liberty wherewith Christ makes free.

The present state of the children is similar to that of their inheritance: "Ourselves also, which have the firstfruits of the spirit, even we ourselves groan within ourselves." Creation has not as yet received any "earnest" or instalment of the future inheritance. How much better is our state who have received the firstfruits of the Spirit? Analogous statements to this are found in other scriptures, particularly in Eph. 1:11–14, which presents many points of resemblance. There we read that the Gentile believers were, when they believed, "sealed with that Holy Spirit of promise, *Who is the earnest of our inheritance* until the redemption of the purchased possession unto the praise of His glory." In 2 Cor. 1:21, 22, are the words: "God, Who hath also sealed us, and given *the earnest of the Spirit* in our hearts "; and in Chapter 5 of the same epistle we read that in this tabernacle, or tent (the mortal body) we "groan being burdened," looking to the time when mortality shall be swallowed up of life. And then follow the words: "Now He that hath wrought us for the self same thing is God, *Who also hath given unto us. the earnest of the Spirit*" (verses 4, 5).

The "earnest" or "firstfruits" is an instalment and sample of what is to follow. Thus we learn that the children of God *have received already* a part of their inheritance, in the Spirit of Promise, Who was promised aforetime to "as many as the Lord our God shall call" (Acts 2:39).

CHAPTER V.

The First Fruits of the Spirit.

(Rom. 8:23.)

Although we have received the firstfruits of the Spirit, nevertheless we groan within ourselves. Or possibly it would be more accurate to say that it is because of the presence and activity of the Spirit within us that we groan within ourselves. It is the Spirit of God who imparts to us the knowledge of the real condition of things at the present time. It is He Who causes us to understand that sin has made havoc of mankind, bringing him into bondage to the dominion of death; that creation also has been put in subjection to vanity, and brought into the bondage of corruption; and that even we ourselves, though delivered from the dominion of sin, and united with the living Christ at God's right hand, are nevertheless appointed for the present time to "wait" in the mortal body, and to suffer with a suffering creation. Thus it is by the Spirit that we can groan, even as the Lord Himself when on earth in the scene where death had brought separation and grief, "groaned in the Spirit and was troubled" (John 11:33). And again, in like manner as the Apostle says "we groan *within ourselves*," so also it is written of Him, " Jesus therefore again groaning *in Himself* cometh to the grave " (John 11:38).

The natural man hears nothing and knows nothing

36

of the groans of creation. He cannot groan in himself
over a state of things whereof he knows nothing. Nor
can the children of God enter into this fellowship of
the sufferings of Christ until they have taken the separated place with Him, outside all the doings, the honours,
the pleasures, the money-getting and other pursuits
and vanities of this present evil age. Alas! how few of
the children of God have heeded the clear teaching of
God's Word and Spirit on this important theme! And
hence, as the necessary consequence, how little desire
is there among them to know the fellowship of Christ's
sufferings in this respect! And if we would inquire
why there is so little genuine eager waiting for the
adoption, the redemption of our body, shall we not find
the reason to be because of practical unbelief, manifested in ignoring the actual state of creation as described
in the Word of God? Yes, the two things cannot be
separated. Those who ignore the suffering and degraded
state of creation, and who endeavor to find ease, and
satisfaction in it as it now is, cannot possibly be waiting eagerly for the glory that is to be revealed to us.
Only those who, by hearkening to the instruction of God's
Word and Spirit, have become intelligent as to the present condition both of the heirs themselves and of their
inheritance, can stand free of the desire for the things
of this world, waiting in ardent expectation for the
redemption of the purchased possession.

In this matter let creation itself teach us and put us
to shame; for the earnest expectation of the creation
awaits the revealing of the sons of God; whereas many
of those who have "received the Spirit of adoption"
seem to be indifferent to the adoption itself, preferring
apparently to derive what satisfaction and enjoyment

they can extract from the creation in its present suffering condition. Alas for those who are "lovers of pleasures more than lovers of God," and who seek their pleasures in a creation that is groaning in pain!

The link between the heirs and their inheritance is very close. They partake of the *same experience now* and *hereafter*. Now they "groan" together and together "wait," in "hope." Then creation will share "the glory of the sons of God," when they shall be "manifested."

The Spirit not only gives us to know and to be in sympathy with the real state of the creation, but also supplies the power whereby we may with patience wait for the hope that is set before us. The righteousness that is "by faith" has a "hope" that pertains to it. This is clear from Chapter 5:1-5. But the things promised, and which constitute the hope of righteousness by faith, are of such a nature, transcending all human experience and the powers of the imagination, that our unaided minds could not form a conception of them (1 Cor. 2:9, 10). So, in this respect as in others, "the Spirit also helpeth our infirmities," revealing to us "the substance of things hoped for," and causing us to know the certainty óf the promised inheritance. So it is written in Gal. 5:5. "For we, *through the Spirit*, do *wait* for the hope of righteousness by faith." It requires something more than human power to maintain in reality the attitude and behavior of one who awaits confidently an event whose arrival is promised though the time thereof be unknown. So those who wait for the hope of righteousness do so "through the Spirit." He supplies strength for that patient endurance which characterizes those who truly have "hope."

And this is the practical outcome which is the object of the portion of Scripture now before us, and of this part of the ministry of the Spirit. It is the purpose of God that His children should *have hope;* that is to say should have it *consciously* and *continuously*, so that it may exert an abiding effect upon their conduct. It is most needful that they should have it; for "every man that *hath this hope* (to be like Christ) set on Him, purifieth himself, even as He is pure " (1 John 3:3). Scriptural "hope" connects its possessor with the coming age of glory, and in corresponding measure delivers him from the things of this present evil age. The things written aforetime concerning the reproaches of Christ, which we are now called upon to share, were written for *our instruction*, to the end that we, *through endurance*, and the comfort (encouragement) of the Scriptures " MIGHT HAVE HOPE " (Rom. 15:3, 4). That is, might have it *now*. For hope is a *present possession*, and is in contrast with the things hoped for, which things themselves are *future*.

As faith connects the believer's heart with a risen, living Christ now at God's right hand, so hope connects his heart with a coming Lord Who is to appear unto salvation. Faith looks upward; hope looks onward. Hope, moreover, is, by its very nature, a thing that can be of value *only* in a state where there are trials to be endured. If we had possession of the things hoped for, there would no longer be any hope, or any need of it. "Hope that is seen is not hope: for what a man seeth why doth he yet hope for?" This characteristic of hope greatly enhances its value and importance; for whatever purpose of God for us is to be served by hope, must be accomplished *now*, while the adoption is yet future. Let us clearly understand this, in order that we may be diligent to

lay firm hold of the hope that is set before us, and also to
" *hold fast* the confidence and the rejoicing of the hope
firm to the end " (Heb. 6:18, 3:6).

Hope then is the present representation and confident
anticipation of the salvation that is yet future, of which
the Apostle says later on (Chapter 13:11) that it is now
"nearer than when we believed." "For we were *saved*
by (or in) hope." Scripture speaks of salvation, in the
complete sense of being delivered from all evil and being
brought into a scene of blessedness, as a thing yet future.
It is ours now " in hope," though as a matter of experience
we still wait for it, seeing it not.   Hope is the believer's
helmet (1 Thess. 5:8) as he looks up and lifts up his
head, knowing that his redemption draws near (Luke
22:28). And the proof that we really have this hope
is that we patiently, with victorious endurance of all
trials and afflictions, *wait for* the promised salvation.
For "if we (really) hope for that we see not, then do we
with patience wait for it."

CHAPTER VI.

The Adoption.

(Rom. 8:23.)

What then is the "ADOPTION" for which we await amid the trials of this groaning creation?

The word "adoption" is found in the Scriptures five times. Three of these occurrences are in Romans (Chapter 8, verses 15 and 23, and Chapter 9, verse 4); one is in Galatians, (Chapter 4, verse 5) and one in Ephesians (Chapter 1, verse 5).

According to modern usage the word "adoption" signifies the act of bringing into the family a child of other parentage. But that does not represent accurately the thought expressed in the original word. Those who are made the children of God do not become such by adoption in that sense. On the contrary they are "*born* of God." (John 1:13; Jam. 1:18; 1 Pet. 1:3; 1 John 5:1). Nor does the adoption signify the new birth. This is evident from the fact that they who are already the children of God, born of the Spirit, and who have spiritual intelligence to cry "Abba, Father," are yet "waiting for the adoption." The adoption then is *future*.

In Rom. 9:4, 5, there is a list of things which, by the sovereign will of God, were bestowed upon Israelites. At the head of that list stands "the adoption." So we see that, in the purpose of God, the adoption pertained to *Israel;* and this was already revealed in the Old Testament Scriptures. It was one of " *their* spiritual things " (Rom. 15:27) though now in Christ it is shared by believing Gentiles. This point is interesting and important, and we shall presently refer to some O. T. Scriptures where the adoption seems to have been foretold.

The word itself rendered by the English word "adoption," is compounded of two Greek words, one signifying " *a son* " (i.e., a mature son—not an infant, or merely a child or offspring, for which other Greek words are used), and the other a verb meaning (among other meanings) "*to place.*" Thus we get the idea of the act of a father placing his adult son in a position of honour and dignity appropriate to his relationship, and expressive of the father's love. This idea is doubtless what the Scriptures intend to convey by the word "adoption." Therefore, we may take it to mean the *full accomplishment of the Father's purpose in the glorifying of those whom He has called to the place of sons, in association with His own Son.* This is clearly stated in verses 28–30. There we read of those whom God has "called according to His *Purpose* "; and that wonderful purpose is declared in verses 29 and 30, namely, that they should be conformed to the image of His Son, to the end that He might be the FIRSTBORN among many brethren. And the purpose will not be completed until the "called" ones are not only "justified," but also "glorified."

The adoption then is nothing less than the glorious prospect placed before the sons of God, in all the fulness of what the Father's love has planned. For we should not lose sight of the fact that the adoption, and all that it involves, is but the complete unfolding of that love of God, towards us, which He commends. "He that spared

not His own Son, but gave Him up for us all (all who are
the called according to His purpose) how shall He not,
WITH HIM also freely give us all things?"—the adoption included (verse 32).

The prominent and most blessed feature of the adoption is the association of the glorified sons of God with
"His own Son." The firstborn is the ruler of the father's
house. So Christ, the Firstborn, occupies the place
of honour and authority over the Father's household.
It is a part of the honour and glory awaiting Him that
He should have under Him "many brethren," and
that these should all be "conformed to His image."
Thus we see that the adoption will be the Father's answer
to the expressed desire of the Son: "Father, I will that
they also, whom Thou hast given me, *be with Me where
I am;* that they may behold My glory which Thou hast
given Me: for Thou lovedst Me before the foundation
of the world " (John 17:24). This " glory " that has been
"given" Him as the Firstborn,—that is to say the glory
that He has acquired by the accomplishing of His
Father's will in the work of redemption, (as distinguished
from His *inherent* glory, which He had with the Father
before the world was) (John 17:5)—He purposes to
share with His co-heirs; for He says: "And the glory
which Thou gavest Me I have given them, that they may
be one, even as We are One " (John 17:22).

᠁The words "they whom Thou hast given Me "; and
the words "that they may be *one* even as We are One,"
connect the foregoing Scriptures with Hebrews 2; where
we read that "both He that sanctifieth and they who
are sanctified are all of *one,*" that is, of one nature as
begotten of God, and embraced in the one purpose of
the Father's love: "For which cause He is not ashamed

to call them brethren, saying, I will declare Thy Name unto My brethren; and again, Behold, I and *the children which God hath given Me* " (verses 11, 13). The children are God's children, begotten of God, and "given" into the care of His Firstborn.

The adoption is not named in this passage in Hebrews, but it is clearly indicated there. The purpose of God is stated in verse 10, namely, "bringing *many sons* unto *glory*." The "many sons" are the "many brethren" of Rom. 8:29; for we are told expressly that Christ is not ashamed to call them "brethren." And "glory" is the ultimate and predestinated state of those many brethren, it being also declared in Rom. 8:30 that they shall be "glorified." Moreover, the words "Behold, I and the children which God hath given Me " bring before the mind a grand presentation scene. They are words indicative of triumph and exultation—words which announce with joy and intense satisfaction the completion of a mighty purpose. He who presents the children to His Father presents them in such a state that He is not ashamed of them before the Father's searching eye; and He does not fear to call attention to them, as well as to Himself, and in association with Himself: "Behold, I and the children." All are there, and all are like Himself. For He is able to present them "faultless before the presence of His glory with exceeding joy " (Jude 24).

We may not bring out here the many points of correspondence between this passage in Hebrews and that in Rom. 8. The reader whose heart is stirred by this subject will seek and find them for himself. But we would point out that according to Hebrews 2 the presentation of the children of God is to take place in connection with the fulfilment of the 8th Psalm, when creation ("the world, or habitable earth, to come") shall be placed under subjection to the Son of Man (Heb. 2:5-8). That will be, of course, when (in the words of Rom. 8:21) creation shall be "delivered from the bondage of corruption." What a blessed exchange for creation, from being "subject to vanity," to be placed in subjection to the Son of God, and His many brethren!

We would also call attention to the fact that the Hebrews passage has to do with the "Heir of all things" and with the "heirs of salvation;" and also to the fact that the prospect here placed before the children of God is declared to be "the hope set before us" (Heb. 3:6; 6:18, 19). These are additional links with the 8th of Romans.

In Hebrews much emphasis is laid upon the responsibility resting on those who have received the remission of their sins (1:3; 10:18, etc.) and to whom "the promise" has been given. These are exhorted to use all diligence to enter into the promised rest, lest any should come short of it. The matter of responsibility of the pardoned sinner is not presented in Romans, which deals with the *purpose of God*, whereof no part could fail. Therefore, the question of the responsibility of the saints with respect to the revealed purpose and will of God for them does not come within the scope of these brief comments. Nevertheless, we would earnestly exhort our fellow-saints, being in constant need of the like exhortation ourselves, to pay earnest heed to the many solemn warnings addressed to us by the Spirit of grace in the letter to the Hebrews.

In Galatians 4 the "adoption" is mentioned in a passage that is full of interest. It appears there, as also in Romans, that the announcement of the adoption is part of the gospel message to Gentiles, as well as to Jews. We have seen that the adoption pertained to the Jews. It was not revealed before the coming of Jesus Christ that Gentiles were to share in the " spiritual things " of the Jews. But that fact (which had previously been a " mystery ") was revealed, not to Paul only, but unto " His (Christ's) holy apostles and prophets by the Spirit" (Eph. 3:5, 6). We shall come to the subject of the " mystery " in Romans 11 and 16, so will not now enlarge upon it. The chief feature of Paul's ministry was to announce among the nations of the world the good news that believing Gentiles were admitted to the covenants and promises, which originally pertained to Israel, including the promise of the Spirit, and were made *fellow heirs*, and of the *same body*, and joint-partakers of *God's promise in Christ* (Eph. 3:6). The word " fellow heirs " connects directly with the subject of the adoption.

It was agreed among the apostles in conference at Jerusalem that Paul and Barnabas should go to the heathen (Gentiles), while Peter and the other apostles should go to the circumcision; Paul having gone to Jerusalem expressly to communicate to them the Gospel which he preached among the Gentiles (Gal. 2:2, 9). It is well to note this because of the impression which seems to prevail in some quarters that Paul preached a different gospel from Peter. Of course this could not be, else one of them would be preaching "another gospel," and be liable to anathema (Gal. 1:7, 8). Paul's gospel, moreover, was not preached to Gentiles only but "to the Jew first" (Rom. 1:16); and on the other hand Peter was the first one to whom the "mystery" was clearly revealed, and who was sent on a special mission to the house of Cornelius (Acts 10) to preach the gospel to Gentiles, according to the mystery, and was chosen to be the human instrument by which the "gift of the Holy Spirit" was bestowed upon them (Acts 15:7).

A careful comparison of the doctrine of 1 Peter with that of Ephesians will reveal so many and so important correspondence, as will effectually dispel the idea that Paul ministered to Gentiles truth differing from that which Peter ministered to Jews. Moreover, Paul declared that, in his preaching, he witnessed to both small and great, "saying none other things than those which the *prophets* and *Moses* did say should come" (Acts 26:22). For the gospel had been "promised afore by the prophets" (Rom. 1:2); though it was a mystery that its privileges were to be shared by Gentiles. Accordingly, in writing to the Galatians, Paul explains the state in which the Jews were, prior to the coming of Christ, in respect to "the inheritance," saying that they had been kept, or safeguarded, under law, as it were in an antechamber, until the time or era of grace, that is, of justifying by faith, which was yet to be revealed. The law was placed over them as a pedagogue is placed over minor children (Gal. 3:18–25). The "inheritance," however, did not come by means of the law, but by promise; for "God gave it to Abraham by promise." Hence the Jews, so long as they were under law, were in the condition of minor children, though they were heirs. "For the heir as long as he is a child (*lit.* an infant or minor) differeth nothing from a servant, though he be lord of all, but is under tutors and governors until the time appointed of the Father" (Gal. 4:1, 2). "Even so," says Paul, "we (Jews) when we were children (minors) were in bondage under the elements of the world. But when the fulness of the time was come, God sent forth His Son, made of woman, made under the law, to redeem them that were under the law (Jews) that *we might receive* THE ADOPTION" (verses 3–5).

So the adoption, which has to do with the inheritance promised to Abraham, remained in abeyance to await redemption by the Son of God, to the end that those who had the promises ("Israelites, to whom pertaineth . . . *the promises*," Rom. 9:4) might receive the adoption. The Jews could never have received the adoption so long as they remained under law. During that period they were "infants," that is, minor children. This Scripture, therefore, furnishes additional proof that the "adoption" is not the new birth, but has to do with the estate of full-grown sons.

The case of Gentile believers was different from that of the Jews in this respect, namely, that God had no dealings with them before the era of grace. They did not enter into the state of sons by way of the intermediate state of minors. To them Paul says "For *ye* (Gentiles in contrast with Jews) *are* sons of God, by faith in Christ Jesus. . . . and if ye be Christ's then are ye Abraham's seed and heirs according to the promise" (Gal. 3:26, 29; verse 26 should read "sons" not "children"). "And because ye are sons, God hath sent forth the Spirit of His Son into your hearts, crying, Abba, Father. Wherefore, thou (believing Gentile) art no more a servant but a son, and if a son, then an heir of God through Christ" (Gal. 4:6, 7).

Verses 4 and 6 present a contrast that is worthy of special notice. Speaking of the Jews, who were under law, Paul says that God *sent forth His Son* to redeem them that were under the law. But speaking to Gentiles, who were not under law, he says "God hath *sent forth the Spirit of His Son* into your hearts." This is the same Spirit called in Rom. 8:15 the "Spirit of adoption," Who is the earnest, and the pledge to us, of the promised inheritance.

In Ephesians 1 we find the last occurrence of the word "adoption." The God and Father of our Lord Jesus Christ "hath blessed us with all spiritual blessings in heavenly places in Christ, according as He hath chosen us in Him before the foundation of the world, that we should be holy and without blame before Him; in love having predestinated us unto (or for) ADOPTION * by Jesus Christ unto Himself."

This passage tells us that the adoption existed in the purpose or will of God before the foundation of the world. That long cherished purpose is so great in God's eyes that He began to prepare for it before the creation. It is evident, therefore, that even creation itself is subordinate to this mighty purpose, and was undertaken in furtherance of it; and also that all the slow development of the ages has ministered to its accomplishment.

We would note particularly that this purposed "adoption" to which we were predestinated was the offspring of Infinite and Eternal Love. For it was "in love" that God marked us out beforehand unto adoption. This is the "great love wherewith He loved us even when we were dead in sins," of which the Apostle speaks in Chapter 2:4, 5. Thus we see, as in Romans, that the special subject of the adoption is embraced in the larger subject of the Love of God. Moreover, the context in

* The words "of children" found in the A. V. have no place in the text and should be omitted. The words "in love" belong, in our opinion, to the clause that follows, not to that which precedes them.

Ephesians says: "In Whom (Christ) also we have obtained an *inheritance*, being *predestinated* according to the purpose of Him who worketh all things after the counsel of His own will" (verse 11), showing that the predestinated inheritance is closely connected with the adoption. (Compare the expression "whom He did predestinate" in Rom. 8:29, 30.)

Furthermore, we have in the Ephesians passage a reference in this immediate connection to the "hope" of the Gospel, though this is partly concealed in the A. V. by the use of the word "trusted" instead of "hoped." Verses 12 and 13 should read: "That *we* (Jews) should be to the praise of His glory who first hoped in Christ; in Whom *ye* (Gentiles) also have hope, having heard the word of the truth, the Gospel of *your* salvation." Immediately following is the prayer in which the Apostle prays that the saints may get to know what is the *hope* of God's calling. This is "the one hope" of our "calling," common to both Jews and Gentiles who believe (Eph. 4:4).

Again we find in the Ephesians passage the "Spirit of the promise" as the earnest of our inheritance, corresponding to the Spirit of adoption mentioned in Romans: "In whom also, having believed, ye were sealed with that Holy Spirit of the promise (compare Acts 2:33, Gal. 3:14, etc.), which is the earnest of our inheritance until the redemption of the purchased possession" (Eph. 1:12–14).

The words "redemption of the purchased possession" occurring in Ephesians in connection with the adoption, and in connection with the Spirit as an earnest of the inheritance, throw light upon the words in Rom. 8:23. "Ourselves also, who have received the firstfruits of the Spirit. . . . Waiting for the adoption, to wit, the redemption of our body."

The heirs, having received the earnest of the Spirit, are required to "wait" for something which is called in Romans "the adoption, the redemption of our body," and in Ephesians, "the redemption of the purchased possession." We know that redemption is already completed in that the *purchase price*, the blood of the Redeemer, has been paid. But the purchased property has not yet been transferred from the hands of the evil powers that held it in bondage to the hands of the Redeemer. (See Luke 21:28.) This purchased property includes not only redeemed sinners of Adam's race, but the creation also, which yet groans in the bondage of corruption.

The Ephesians passage is also related to Hebrews 2 by the words "that we should be holy and without blame *before Him*." This purpose will be fulfilled when the Captain of our Salvation presents the children whom He has sanctified (i.e., made holy) before the Father's Presence, praising Him in the midst of the great congregation, and saying, "Behold I and the children which God hath given Me." Thus He will present them faultless before the presence of His glory with exceeding joy.

We gather then, from all these Scriptures, that the "adoption" is that great coming event wherein the desire of the Father's heart will be fully satisfied, and the purpose of the ages, which He purposed in Christ Jesus, shall be fully realized, when God shall set before His Face His family of many sons, all conformed in character to the image of His Firstborn, and all sharing His glorious likeness. It is beyond the power of our imagination at its utmost stretch to conceive the displays of divine glory, the outbursts of rejoicing in which creation itself will take part (Ps. 96:11–13), that will accompany the " Manifestation of the sons of God " in the exalted station to which they have been called, and for which they are being prepared.

That formal majestic, and public glorification of the Son of God will be the answer of Heaven to the shame of the cross to which He was condemned on earth. Then He shall indeed see of the travail of His soul and be satisfied; for then He will enter into the fulness of the joy that was set before Him when He endured the cross, despising the shame.

We can readily picture to ourselves what an earthly potentate of great wealth would do on the occasion of installing his only son in the place of honour and authority over his kingdom, what riches he would lavish, and what efforts he would put forth to make the occasion one of magnificent and gorgeous display; and yet we may be sure that this illustration would not even faintly represent what the God and Father of our Lord Jesus Christ will do on the occasion when His own Son, with His co-heirs, shall be installed over the redeemed creation. And if we are able to gain ever so faint a glimpse of the glory of that coming scene, it will surely serve to separate us from all the vanities of this present age, to supply endurance as we patiently wait for the hope that is not seen as yet, and even in times of trial and affliction enable us to say, " I reckon that the sufferings of this present time are not worthy to be compared with the glory which shall be revealed to us."

The various expressions "the glory which shall be

revealed to us" (Rom. 8:18) "the manifestation of the
sons of God" (19), "the liberty of the glory of the
children of God" (21), the "hope" in which we "were
saved," and for which we should "wait" (24, 25); the
time when we shall be conformed to the image of God's
Son, and He shall be "Firstborn among many brethren,"
all of them "glorified" (29, 30), and the "salvation"
that is now "nearer than when we believed" (13:11) all
indicate and have reference to the "adoption" for which
the sons of God are waiting.

CHAPTER VII.

Further Ministries of the Spirit, and Further Meditations on the Love of God.

(Rom. 8:26–39.)

We have before us in Romans 8 some of the varied ministries of the Spirit "Who is given to us." The relation of the Spirit of God to the sons of God appears from the Scriptures already cited, and particularly from the significant expression used by the Lord Himself "the promise of My Father" (Lu. 24:49) and "the promise of the Father" (Acts 1:4). The word "Father" used in this connection, tells us that the Spirit is given to the sons of God as a special expression and "seal" of their holy relationship with the Father, and as the "power" bestowed upon them for the purpose of maintaining them, amid this scene of trial, danger and defilement, in a holy "walk," and in communion with the Father and the Son.

What properly characterizes the sons of God is that they are "led by the Spirit of God." They are not to be led by the imaginations of their own hearts, or the impulses of their own minds, to walk according to the course of this world; but they are to be led by a living, Divine Being, present, though unseen, "Whom the world cannot receive because it seeth Him not " (John 14:17). Those children of God who *will* to be led by the Spirit, and who voluntarily yield to His guidance, can count upon Him to fulfil every detail of His most gracious, and most important ministry. We can do nothing according to the will of God or in furtherance of His purpose except "through the Spirit."

We have seen that the Spirit awakens in the child of God a consciousness of his relation to the Father, which finds expression in the cry "Abba," the first syllables—*ab-ba*—which a child's lips learn to utter; that He makes known the fact of heirship as resulting from sonship; that He shows us that our inheritance is not in the creation as it now is, and puts us in sympathy with the suffering creature; and that He empowers us with endurance to wait patiently for the "adoption," *i.e.,* the hope that is set before us. In all these important matters the Spirit helps our infirmities.

Our infirmities include ignorance of what things we ought to pray for (Rom. 8:26). What is more important in the life of a son of God than prayer? The teaching and example of the Lord show that prayer is a matter of the very highest importance. In that exercise we take the place of utter dependance upon God, giving Him His rightful place as the only One who can accomplish what is good. The bowed knees express the cessation of human activity, and the clasped hands tell of the impotence of the arm of flesh. In prayer we call Omnipotence into action, while being engaged ourselves in that which cannot be observed and praised of men.

But it is essential that prayer should be intelligent. It should be the expression of the knowledge of the will and purpose of God. We need to know what things we ought to pray for; and the fact is that we do *not* know what things we ought to pray for. To supply this knowledge is one of the ministries of the Spirit, so that we may pray in harmony with the Father's purpose, not only in general, but in minute detail, according to varying conditions from day to day. To this end the Spirit Himself makes intercession for us, that we "might be filled with the knowlege of His (God's) will in all wisdom and spiritual understanding" (Col. 1:9), so that we may be able to pray always " with all prayer and supplication *in the Spirit*" (Eph. 6:18). Such as have ever addicted themselves to prayer know by happy experience what it is to have the help of the Spirit in bringing before the eyes of the heart the things for which we "ought" to pray.

Failure to count upon the ministry of the Spirit always leads to the adoption of some human substitute. The professing church, with its manifold man-made contrivances, bears sad testimony to the lack of faith in the presence and power of the Spirit of God in the congregations of the saints. Hence formularies of prayer have largely taken the place of "praying in the Holy Ghost." That the two are incompatible is manifest; for the rigid "form" of prayer, devised by unknown men who have long passed away, may not be changed, in even a small particular, whatever might be the desire of the living and present Spirit. The stated words must be said, in the stated order, at the stated times, regardless of "the mind of the Spirit." Thus has a grievous yoke been fastened upon the necks of the people. Forms are dead things; whereas "the Spirit is life." The Spirit does not lead the children of God to address their Father in set forms of words, however stately and dignified. No children speak to a father in that way.

The Spirit Himself makes intercession *for* us with groanings that cannot be uttered, which seems to signify the intensity of the Spirit's intercession. The Son of God, now at God's right hand, "also maketh intercession for us " (verse 34). Thus the Father has provided for His children, during the time of their need and exposure to danger, with two mighty Intercessors. One of These is here with us and the Other is on high, in the place of supreme honour and authority.

Although the Spirit's intercession is with groanings inexpressible, nevertheless, He who searches the hearts (see Rev. 2:23) knows what is the mind of the Spirit, because He maketh intercession for the saints according to God. Thus three things are stated concerning the intercession of the Spirit *for* us, namely that it is intense, that it is known on high, and that it is " according to God." This should give confidence to our hearts.

When we are undergoing tribulation, pressure, or pain, we might suppose that the intercession of the Spirit on our behalf was unavailing, or might we be so unbelieving as to doubt the unchanging character of the love of God. But we know by the teaching of the Spirit that " all things," however painful and distressing they may be, "work together for good, to them that love God, to them who are the called according to His purpose " (verse 28). All sickness, sorrow, poverty, loss, and other suffering, are pressed into service by the Father, and are compelled to work for the benefit of His children, in the furtherance of His great purpose for them, the final outcome being that they should be conformed to the image of His Son and be " glorified " with the glory which God has given Him. The apostle Paul had this knowledge of the purposes which God accomplishes through experiences that are painful and distressing in the extreme; and this knowledge sustained him through unparalleled trials and sufferings. He knew what it was to be "troubled on every side, yet not distressed; perplexed, but not in despair, persecuted but not forsaken; cast down but not destroyed " (2 Cor. 4:8, 9). He knew what it was to be "in afflictions, in necessities, in distresses, in stripes, in imprisonments, in tumults, in labours, in watchings, in fastings" (2 Cor. 6:4, 5). Yet knowing that all things work together for good to them that love God, he could speak of it all as a light affliction, saying: "For our light affliction, which is but for a moment, worketh for us a far more exceeding and eternal weight of GLORY, while we look not at the things which are seen (the afflictions and trials) but at the things that are not seen " (the adoption and the glory of the coming day).

"What shall we then say to these things?" (verse 31). Shall we speak of anything as being "against us"? We often do so think and speak when we find ourselves in trouble, difficulty, or suffering. Has not God clearly revealed to us that, however much these things may seem to be "against us," He compels all things to work for our good? But beyond all that, God Himself is "for us." All that God is, infinite in love, in wisdom, and in might, is for us. The Son of God intercedes for us, and the Spirit of God intercedes for us. We are even necessary to the carrying out of God's supremest purpose. Who or what then can be against us? True, the enemies of God set themselves, and put forth all their efforts to defeat His purpose; but, to His praise and their shame, they only succeed after all in furthering that purpose. For of a truth both Herod and Pontius Pilate, with the Gentiles, and the people of Israel were gathered together against the Christ of God, but when they had done their worst, according to the counsels of their own hearts, they succeeded only in doing what God's hand, and God's counsel determined before to be done (Acts 4:27, 28). And thus it will ever be with all that rises up in opposition to the purposes of God.

Shall we doubt the purpose of God to bring us into His glory, and to give us the things promised to His heirs? Here is a fact that puts an end to such a question. " He that spared not His own Son, but delivered Him up for us all, how shall He not, with Him, also freely give us all *things?*" How would it be possible for Him to withhold anything from those for whom He delivered up His own Son?

Shall we doubt our justification, and question whether there may not yet be some charge against us which the Accuser can raise? Let this be the answer "It is God that justifieth." No flaw can be found in His work. Whoever lays anything to the charge of God's elect accuses not them, but Him; for He has made their justification His work.

Shall we fear condemnation? (ver. 34). Who is there to condemn us? All judgment has been committed to the Son (John 5:22). Will He condemn us? He is the very One that died for us; but more than that He is risen again. His death was " for our offences " and His rising again was " for our justification." (Rom. 4:25.) Will He condemn for the offences for which He died, and concerning which we have been justified and cleared, as proved by His resurrection? But more than that, how could He condemn those for whom He intercedes?

Who shall separate us from the love of Christ? (verses 35–37). Can anything that may befall us here cut us off from His love? Can tribulation, or distress, or persecution, or famine, or nakedness, or peril, or sword, even though we be among those who, for His sake, are killed all the day long, and are accounted as sheep for the slaughter? Even though we should be killed for His sake, shall we suppose that it means the failure of His love for us? Surely not, for even in the extremities of human sufferings we are more than conquerors THROUGH HIM THAT LOVED US. Even those extreme things shall not overcome us; but, through Him Who loves us, we shall overcome them. Indeed we shall be "more than conquerors." A conqueror merely achieves a victory, often with severe loss to himself, over his adversaries. But, through Him Who loves us, those things are not merely overcome, but are compelled to work together for our good.

The blessed and glorious conclusion of the whole matter (verses 38, 39), is that no created thing shall have the ability to separate us from the love of God, which love has its supreme expression and its eternal abiding place "in Christ Jesus our Lord." Death cannot do it, though death is the great separator. Life cannot do it, nor unseen beings, good or bad, whether angels, or principalities or powers, though they "excel in strength." Things present, however grievous, cannot do it; nor the unknown things to come, whatever their nature may be. No height is high enough, and no depth deep enough to take us out of the embrace of Infinite and Eternal Love.

Such is the Love of God. Let us note with wondering and worshipping hearts the things that are here recorded of it.

It is made known by the Holy Spirit to our hearts. His presence there is the evidence of it.

God commends it, in that the nature and the measure of it are seen in His giving His own Son to die for us, and that while we were yet sinners.

It brings us into the close and holy relation of "sons" to the Father.

His Spirit causes us to know ourselves in this relation to Him, bearing witness with our spirit that we are the children of God.

This relationship, which is the fruit of love, assures us as to the future, delivering us from the bondage of fear, and enabling us to rejoice in hope of the glory of God.

This relationship of love necessarily makes us also heirs of God.

Though we may be called upon to endure trials and sufferings now, the Father's love turns all these things to our profit. For if we endure chastening God dealeth with us as with sons; for what son is he whom the Father chasteneth not? " For whom the Lord *loveth* He chasteneth " (Heb. 12: 6).

As sons it is our high privilege to know, and to be in accord with, the Father's purpose; and we learn that the central feature of that great purpose is to glorify His Firstborn as Head over His house.

The entire purpose of God sprang from what God Himself is; for "God is Love." Hence all that God is stands for the full accomplishment of His purpose.

We are more than conquerors—even we who in ourselves are "without strength"—but it is solely "through Him that loved us."

And finally, the last door to the entrance of doubt is

closed by the assurance that nothing seen or unseen, present or to come, shall be able to separate us from the Love of God that is in Christ Jesus our Lord.

Thus fittingly closes that part of the Epistle which deals with the great subject of the Love of God.

CHAPTER VIII.

Israel and the "Remnant."
"Their Spiritual Things."

(Rom. 9:1–5.)

The "gospel" reveals that God's purpose at the present time has to do, not with the covenant people of Israel, but with God's family of sons, and that the work of the Son of God, the Intercessor in heaven, and of the Spirit of God, the Intercessor on earth, has for its great object the perfecting of the " many sons," whom God is " bringing unto glory." Moreover, the Scriptures make known that this purpose of God in regard to His own household, is not a new plan, brought forward in consequence of the failure and apostasy of Israel; but is God's original purpose from the very beginning, even " the purpose of the ages which He purposed in Christ Jesus our Lord " (Eph. 3:11).

But the purposes and promises of God, as revealed in the Old Testament Scriptures, were in connection with Israel. Has God then departed from His purposes in respect to Israel? If so, what has become of "the Israel of God " (Gal. 6:16). "Has God cast away His people"? (Rom. 11:1). This is a question that needs to be answered, else our knowledge of God's dealings with men would be very deficient, and there would appear to be variableness in God, "with Whom is

63

no variableness nor shadow of turning " (James 1:17). Therefore, we find in Romans 9, 10 and 11, a portion of Scripture which answers the foregoing question, and in which it is declared that "the gifts and calling of God are without repentance " (change of purpose on God's part. Rom. 11:29).

We deem it very important that the people of God should pay earnest heed to these chapters, in order that they may have the satisfaction of seeing that the work of the gospel is not an interruption of, or a digression from, God's purpose which was announced to Israel and in their behalf; but that it is, on the contrary, the carrying forward of that pre-announced purpose toward its full accomplishment.   To be sure, the purpose of God, now that the era of " shadows " is passed away and the " true light now shineth," is seen to be far more vast in its scope, and more glorious in its consummation, than was revealed to the prophets of old.   Nevertheless, the purpose of God in Christ was revealed by God to His servants the prophets; "into whom it was revealed" also (says the Apostle Peter) "that not unto themselves, but unto us, did they minister the things (those self-same things) which are now reported unto you, by them that have PREACHED THE GOSPEL unto you, with the Holy Ghost sent down from heaven " (1 Peter 1:12).   So that the preaching of the Gospel in the power of the Holy Ghost sent down from heaven is the carrying out of the very things which God revealed to the prophets concerning " the sufferings of Christ and the glories that should follow."   And with this agree also the words of Paul, who writes of "the Gospel of God, which He had promised afore by His prophets in the Holy Scriptures" (Rom. 1:1, 2).

Let us then take careful note of the things which pertained to Israel as stated in Rom. 9:4, 5, namely 1, the adoption; 2, the glory; 3, the covenants; 4, the giving of the law; 5, the service or worship of the true God; 6, the promises; 7, the fathers. Here is a complete series of seven things. And to them is added an eighth, which far surpasses all the others, "And of whom as concerning the flesh CHRIST came, Who is over all, God blessed for ever."

These are the privileges which pertain, in the unchangeable counsels of God, to the Israelites. The Apostle Paul, having these things that pertain to Israel before his eyes, and having the hardened and apostate condition of the mass of the Israelites also before him, was oppressed with the burden of a heavy and continual sorrow. So great was this burden that it could only find adequate expression in the wish that, for the sake of his brethren, his kinsmen according to flesh who are Israelites, he were "anathema from Christ." This forcibly calls to mind the cry that was wrung from the heart of Moses at the time of Israel's apostasy "Oh, this people have sinned a great sin, and have made them gods of gold. Yet now, if Thou wilt forgive their sin—; and if not, blot me, I pray thee, out of Thy book which Thou hast written " (Ex. 32:32). Surely none ever had greater love for Israel than Moses and Paul, between whom there are many resemblances. It was indeed cause for profound grief to a true Israelite that his kinsmen should turn away from such wondrous privileges, bestowed upon them by the sovereign grace of God, thus forsaking " their own mercies " (Jonah 2:8).

What happened historically was this: After the Israelites had been shut up under law for the period determined by God, and when the fulness of the time was come, God sent forth His own Son, the Christ of God, to fulfil all that was written of Him in the volume of the Book. He came to His own possessions, but His own people received Him not home (John 1:11). On the contrary, and as foretold by the prophets, He was despised and rejected by them, cast out and crucified, the charge against Him being that He made Himself the Christ, the Son of God, and hence a King, as clearly stated in Ps. 2:6, 7. (See Luke 22:70, 71 and 23:2.) And when He hung on the cross dying "for THAT NATION" and also in order that "He should gather together in one THE CHILDREN OF GOD that were scattered abroad," (John 11:50–52), they did not recognize Him as the Promised One, undergoing " the suffering pertaining to the Christ," but on the contrary they regarded Him with hatred and aversion as one " stricken of God and afflicted," even as the prophet Isaiah had foretold.

What then? Did that act cause the severance of God's relations with His people Israel? Not so; the same Scripture which contains the solemn statement that "His own (people) received Him not," records also the exceedingly important fact that *some individual Israelites did receive Him* (John 1:11, 12). Therefore, the full purpose of God for Israel is carried out, and all the promises of God (which are yea and amen in Christ) are made good *in those individual Israelites who did receive the Messiah.* Those believing ones constitute " the Israel of God " and " the Remnant."

Among the wondrous "promises" pertaining to Israel is that found in Hosea 1:10. "And it shall come to pass that in the place where it was said unto them: Ye are

not My people, there it shall be'said unto them: Ye are
THE SONS OF THE LIVING GOD."

The apostle John records the fulfilment of this great
promise in the Scripture already cited. "But to *as many
as received Him*, to them gave He power to become THE
SONS OF GOD, even to them that believe on His Name."

Here then we have the beginning of the family
of God, in fulfilment of the distinct promise given in
Hosea. This is expressly stated in Rom. 9:26 where
the foregoing passage of Hosea's prophecy is quoted.

Thus we learn that the family of God, which includes
those who receive His Son, and who believe on His Name,
being " born of God," was composed at the outset *entirely
of Israelites*. The fact that the number of these believing
Israelites was small in comparison with the total number
of the nation, does not in the slightest degree impair the
continuity of God's dealings. Nor does it affect the carrying out of His purpose with respect to Israel. But we
must learn to regard this believing remnant as the real
" Israel," and all the others as not real Israelites. This is
the lesson taught in the chapter now before us, where we
read that "they are not all 'Israel' which are *of* Israel "
(literally "which are *out of* Israel," *i.e.*, were descendants of Israel). That is to say, if we ask where we shall
find "Israel," meaning the Israel of promise and prophecy,
the "Israel of God" to whom all these spiritual blessings
pertained, we are told that Israel in this sense is not the
nation composed of the descendants of Jacob, but it is
this believing company, or " remnant."

This is the prominent truth set forth in Rom. 9–11, and
it should be clearly apprehended by the people of God.
It is elucidated in Chapter 11 by the illustration of the
Olive Tree, which represents Israel. The branches broken

off are the unbelieving Israelites, who are no longer
regarded as belonging to the Israel of God, so far at least
as concerns being in line with the purpose of God which
He is now carrying forward. It is evident that the
branches of a tree which have been broken off are no longer
a part of that tree. And it is also evident that though
but very few of the branches remain on the root, they
nevertheless constitute the real tree. Thus we can
identify in the believing remnant the true " Israel " of the
prophecies.   The few Israelites who have " received "
Jesus Christ are the " natural branches " of the olive
tree.   But God, in His uncovenanted grace, is now
admitting believers from among the Gentiles to all the
benefits secured by the death and resurrection of the
Messiah.   These believing Gentiles are the branches that
are " cut out of the olive tree that is wild by nature,"
and which partake, or perfect equality with the natural
branches, of all the goodness of the tree.   They are,
indeed, as much a part of the tree as the natural branches.
But inasmuch as they owe their position of favour and
blessedness to an unimaginable act of grace and power
on the part of the God of Israel, it becomes them to
" be not high minded, but to fear."

The great point here emphasized is the *continuity* of the
purpose of God, which had been declared in regard to
Israel, and which is now being carried out in the believing
remnant, which is the *real* Israel, and is being extended by
God's sovereign grace, as was always a part of His
counsels, though not previously revealed, to embrace
also believers from among the Gentiles.

This is a very different thing from that which is sometimes taught, and is held by not a few, namely that God
has broken wholly with Israel, and that the church is a

" mystery " whereof there was no hint in the Old Testament Scriptures; and that the present age wherein the church is being formed is a " parenthesis," during which God's dealings with Israel are wholly interrupted. The fact is that the line of God's dealings with His people Israel has not been interrupted at all. It continues straight on without break. Only we are now instructed by the Scripture to recognize those Israelites, who received the Messiah, believing on His Name, as the real " Israel."

We shall do well, therefore, to scrutinize carefully the list of " things " that pertained to the Israelites, which the Apostle calls " their spiritual things " (15:27); because we " Gentiles (who believe) have been made partakers of *their* spiritual things." In contrast with this, it is sometimes taught in the present day that the gospel preached by Paul brings those who believe it into something entirely new, a " mystery " never before revealed. Moreover, we are often told that the blessings promised to Israel are " *earthly*," but that God has " blessed *us* with all *spiritual* blessings in heavenly places." It seems to be supposed by some that earthly blessings cannot be spiritual. That, however, is not the case, and by examining carefully this list we shall learn what is meant in Scripture by " spiritual things."

The " adoption " and the " glory " have been already noticed. We have seen that the adoption was foretold in Hosea 1:10. It is also foretold in Ps. 22:22, where the Spirit of Christ in the prophet, having prophesied the sufferings of Christ on the cross, tells of the glory that should follow, saying, "I will declare Thy Name unto my brethren: in the midst of the congregation will I praise Thee." By Heb. 2:10-13 we learn that this will be fulfilled when Christ presents to the Father the many sons whom He is bringing "unto glory," in a word at the "adoption." From Heb. 2:12 we learn also that Is. 8:18 is another Scripture which foretells the adoption; for there we find the words "Behold, I and the children whom the Lord hath given Me." It is significant that this is part of a prophecy relating expressly to "Immanuel," that is to say, "God with us" (Is. 7:17; 8:8 and 10).

The "covenants" embrace the covenants of God with Abraham, seven in all, and those with David. But the covenant which chiefly concerns us is that known as the "New Covenant." To this new covenant the Lord Jesus referred when, on the night of His betrayal, He gave His disciples the cup after supper saying "Drink ye all of it, for this is My blood of the *new covenant* which is shed for many for the remission of sins " (Matt. 26:27, 28). His people recall this covenant to mind every time they show the Lord's death in the appointed manner (1 Cor. 11:25, 26). This is the covenant whereof Paul says he was made a minister, and which he says is the covenant "of the Spirit," which "giveth life," and the covenant which has "the glory that excelleth" (2 Cor. 3:6-10). This is the "better covenant" whereof the Lord Jesus is the "Surety" (Heb. 7:22) and "the Mediator" (8:6). It is "the everlasting covenant" sealed in His blood (Heb. 13:20).

The chief feature of this new covenant is " the remission of sins " (Matt. 26:28; Heb. 8:6-12, 10:16, 17); and this (the remission of sins) is *the message of the gospel*, which the Risen Christ commanded to be preached in His Name among all *nations* (Luke 24:47). It is the

gospel preached by Peter, and by Paul, and by all the
apostles. Speaking of the gospel message "that Christ
died for our sins according to the Scriptures," etc.,
Paul said he laboured therein more than all the
other apostles, and added "Therefore, whether it were
I or they, so we preached." "So" all the apostles
preached.

Let it then be noted that this spirtual blessing *i.e.,*
the remission of sins—wherewith we have been blessed
in heavenly places in Christ, was at first promised solely
to Jews. It is found in Jer. 31:31-34; and the passage
begins with the words, " Behold, the days come, saith
the Lord, that I will make *a new covenant with the
house of Israel and with the house of Judah*." If,
therefore, we Gentile believers, have a share in this
covenant, it is solely because God, in His infinite grace,
has grafted us in among the natural branches, making
us partakers of the root and fatness of the olive tree.
Let us then "be not high minded, but fear."

The Israelites had also " the giving of the law," which
also is a spiritual blessing; " for we know that the law is
spiritual" (Rom. 7:14). They had also the divinely
appointed " service," (the symbolical system of sacrifices
and worship revealed to Moses at the institution of the
Tabernacle), a service consisting indeed of " shadows,"
but of shadows that all foretold Christ, and pointed
forward to the time when the real worshippers should
worship the Father in spirit and in truth (John 4:23).
Israel had not only the shadows but also the corresponding
reality.

The Israelites had also "the promises," which are
too numerous to mention. But we find references
in Romans and Galatians to the "gospel promised afore,"

to " the promise of the Spirit," and to the promise unto Abraham of an inheritance (see also Heb. 11:13).

The Israelites had also "the fathers"; but the crowning blessing of all, which includes and goes far beyond all the rest, is that of them "as concerning the flesh Christ came, Who is over all, God blessed for ever. Amen."

Such are Israel's "spiritual things."

CHAPTER IX.

"The Election of God."

(Rom. 9:6-33.)

Although the apostle is crushed and depressed as he contemplates the apostasy and blindness of the mass of the Israelites, yet he hastens to say that it is "not as though the Word of God had taken none effect. For they are not all 'Israel' which are of Israel."

To the same effect it is stated in Chapter 2: "For he is not a Jew which is one outwardly; neither is that circumcision which is outward in the flesh; but he is (really) a Jew, which is one inwardly; and (real) circumcision is that of the heart, in the spirit, not in the letter" (Rom. 2:28, 29).

Thus we arrive at the conclusion that the real Israel of prophecy, and of God's purpose, is the little company of those who believed in Christ. " For," asks the apostle, " what if some did not believe,"—even though it be the majority of the nation—" shall their unbelief make the faith of God of none effect? Let it not be " (Rom. 3:3, 4).

Returning to Chapter 9, the apostle further points out (verse 7, 8) that because they are the seed of Abraham it does not follow that they are "children," i.e., children to whom the promise applies. John the Baptist warned the Pharisees and Sadducees not to rest upon the thought that they had Abraham for their father; "for" said he,

73

"I say unto you that God is able of these stones to raise up children unto Abraham."

So also the Lord, speaking to the Pharisees said, "If ye were Abraham's children ye would do the works of Abraham" (John 8:39). The real children of Abraham, "before Him Whom he believed, even God Who quickeneth the dead," (Rom. 4:16, 17) are *those who believe on the Son of God*, as it is written "Know ye, therefore, that they which are *of faith*, the same are the *children of Abraham;*" and again, "So then they which be *of faith* are blessed with faithful Abraham"; and again, "And if ye be Christ's, then are ye Abraham's seed, and heirs according to the promise" (Gal. 3:7, 9, 29).

The effect of the coming of Christ was to cause a separation between those who are equally the posterity of Abraham. This appears from the words of Rom. 9:7, "In Isaac, shall thy seed be called," quoted from Gen. 21:18. Thus it appears that Abraham's act in casting out the bond woman and her son, at the Lord's command, was prophetic of the cutting off of many of the natural braches of the olive tree. For all the numerous descendants of Ishmael are the natural children of Abraham.

This word of the Lord also brings before us an exceedingly important principle of divine action, namely the choice, or calling, or "election" of God. Literally the words are "but in Isaac shall be *called to thee* a seed." That is to say, the seed of Abraham to whom the promises were to be fulfilled were not "they which are the children of the flesh" (9:8). They to whom God gave the right to become His children "were born not of blood, nor of the will of the flesh, nor of the will of man, but of God." Man may will never so earnestly and may run never so vigorously, it is of no avail in this matter. The "calling" or "choice" is of God, and is in His hand alone. He chooses whom He wills to be the vessels of His mercy, whereof all are alike undeserving.

The words of Jehovah, "In Isaac shall be called to thee a seed," are quoted also in Heb. 11:17, where we read: "By faith, Abraham, when he was tried, offered up Isaac: and he that had received the promises offered up his only begotten son, of whom it was said, That in Isaac shall thy seed be called; accounting that God was able to raise him up, even from the dead; from whence also he received him in a figure."

Isaac thus typifies the Son of God, offered up and received again by His Father from the dead. In Him (Christ, the Risen Lord) the children of the promise are "called," they being counted as dead, buried, and raised with Christ (Rom. 6:4–6).

The case of Rebecca furnishes another illustration of the principle of God's sovereign choice. For before the children, Esau and Jacob, were born, neither having done any good or evil, God made choice of Jacob, the younger, electing that through Jacob, not through Esau, His purpose should be carried out. God foreknew the children of Isaac, not only while in their mother's womb, but before even the world was founded. God's election antedates creation (Eph. 1:5). God can survey our hearts and lives before we are born, just as well as after we die.

"What shall we say then? Is there unrighteousness with God?" Is there the slightest injustice in God's act in choosing some and not others? Certainly not. God's foreknowledge of those whom He chooses is one reply to this suggestion (which rises in the minds of some).

For the Scriptures clearly state that God does not exercise arbitrarily His prerogative of choosing those whom He will admit into His family, but that He chooses all who believe the Gospel. Nevertheless, it is most needful for us to apprehend clearly the humbling truth that our being chosen of God is *solely* a matter of His sovereign grace, and is not due to any virtue or any acts of ours. Even Abraham had *nothing* to boast of before God.

So the answer which this passage gives to the suggestion of injustice on God's part is this: "For He saith unto Moses, *I will* have mercy on whom *I will* have mercy, and *I will* have compassion on whom *I will* have compassion. So then it (the election by God of His children is not of him that willeth, nor of him that runneth, but of God that showeth mercy."

Let it be specially noticed then that the act of election or the exercise of God's "will," four times mentioned in the foregoing verse, is an act of *mercy*. Israel had *all* sinned in turning from God to worship the golden calf. Therefore *all* deserved to be cut off. Hence we should praise the mercy that spared some of the guilty undeserving ones, no matter what may be the principle upon which God chooses those whom He will spare. But, in fact, and as already said, God chooses for vessels of mercy in this age, those who believe on His Son. For "the scripture hath concluded *all under sin*, that the promise by faith of Jesus Christ might be GIVEN TO THEM THAT BELIEVE " (Gal. 3:22).

If, therefore, any reader of these pages should be exercised over the question "Am I one of the elect children of the promise, born of God?" he has only to ask himself "do I believe in Jesus Christ, God's Son?"

"For whosoever believeth that Jesus is the Christ *is born of God*" (1 John 5:1). "To them gave He power to become the sons of God, even to them that *believe on His name*. Who are born of God" (John 1:12, 13).

Thus it is that "the purpose of God according to election" is caused to stand, "not of works, but of Him that calleth."

The case of Pharaoh, which has perplexed many, is next cited as an instance in which God acted according to His sovereign will, in order to display His power and His mercy. "For the Scripture saith unto Pharaoh, Even for this same purpose have I raised thee up, that I might show My power in thee, and that My Name might be declared throughout all the earth. Therefore hath He mercy on whom He will, and whom He will He hardeneth."

Let us be careful that, in every case, no matter what its circumstances, we justify God, for He is righteous in *all* His acts. Thus we show ourselves the children of wisdom, for "Wisdom is justified of her children." We need not, therefore, seek to find ground for justifying God in hardening the heart of Pharaoh. The text says that God's dealings with Pharaoh were acts of mercy. Not necessarily mercy to Pharaoh, though God certainly was merciful to him in not cutting him off the first time he resisted the command of God to let His people go. Pharaoh was the greatest ruler in all the world, and already he was by his own disobedience to God's express command, "fitted to destruction." Therefore, God made use of this mighty monarch as a "vessel to wrath," through whom God's own power might be shown, in order that His Name might be declared throughout all the earth. Thus the case of Pharaoh has served the purpose of world-wide instruction for all succeeding generations of men.

Should any one be disposed to question, as many have done, the equity of God's dealings with Pharaoh in hardening his heart, it is a sufficient reply to such to say that God has the same right over the lump of sinful humanity in His hands that the potter has over the clay whereof he fashions vessels for various uses, some honourable, some dishonourable. Certainly it does not lie in the mouth of the creature to say to the Creator, "Why hast Thou made me thus?"

But in this case, God has been pleased to give the reason for His way of dealing with the potentate of Egypt. The reason was that God willed, for the furtherance of His merciful plan, "to show His wrath, and to make His power known." It was for the good of His human creatures in general that He should do so. In doing this He did no wrong to Pharaoh. On the contrary, He "endured with *much long suffering*" that vessel of wrath. For God gave him many opportunities to yield to His command, instead of cutting him down at the first act of resistance. Pharaoh first "hardened" (or *strengthened*, which is the significance of the word,) his own will to resist the command of God. Thereafter, God Himself (possibly by the mere withholding of punishment, and by repeated acts of mercy in removing the plagues) hardened Pharaoh's will for still further resistance, until the conditions for the final display of God's power were brought about.

But the display of God's wrath and power were not the end in themselves at which He was aiming. His main and ultimate purpose, to which the display of His power and wrath contributed, was "that He might make known the riches of His glory on the vessels of mercy, which He had afore prepared unto glory, even us, whom He hath called, not of the Jews only, but also of the Gentiles " (verses 23, 24).

Here we find another clear announcement of the purpose of God in respect to those "whom He hath called," *i.e.*, the election. These also are " vessels " for His sovereign use and service. Not vessels of wrath, but of mercy. Not fitted by themselves, but prepared by God Himself. God had need of such, because He purposes to make a public display to all the intelligences of the universe of "the riches of His glory" (cf. Eph. 1:18 and 3:16). For that use He chose and prepared such as it pleased Him to choose out of the fallen and ruined race of human beings. With that choice the creature has *absolutely nothing to do*.

Vessels are for the use of the one who makes them. God willed, for His own glory and for the good of men, to show His wrath and make known His power. For this purpose He made use of vessels *already fitted to destruction*. He also willed to make known to all His intelligent creatures the riches of His glory; and for this high purpose He is preparing vessels of mercy, even those whom He has been pleased to call. Let us rejoice in the grace that has revealed this purpose to us, that we might enjoy the sons' privilege of knowing what the Father is doing.

The prophecy of Hosea is now cited as foretelling the "calling" of these vessels of mercy. In that prophecy are found the words " I will call them My people which were not My people, and her beloved which was not beloved." Some expositors hold the view that the period when Israel is "Lo-Ammi" to God (*i.e.*, "not My people") is this present age; and that at the end of this age Israel will again be called "Ammi—My people." But it is evident that the "Lo-Ammi" period of Israel began at the captivity of Babylon, and ended when the believing remnant, the real Israel, received the Messiah, and became the people of God. For God commanded Hosea to say to the Israelites, "Ye are not My people and I will not be your God" (Hos. 1:9). This proves that the Lo-Ammi period had already begun. On the other hand the Apostle Peter, in writing to the believing Israelites who had become the children of God, born again of the incorruptible seed of the Word of God, through the Gospel, shows that the Lo-Ammi period had run its course, saying, "Ye are a chosen generation, a royal priesthood, an holy nation, a *peculiar people*. . . which *in time past* (the Lo-Ammi period being then already past) *were not* a people; but are *now* the people of God; which *had not* obtained mercy, but *now have* obtained mercy" (1 Pet. 2:9, 10). Since Peter quotes the words of Hosea's prophecy it is beyond all question that the Lo-Ammi period was at an end when Peter's letter was written.

Thus the purpose of God has its fulfilment in the remnant according to the election of grace. As Isaiah said "Though the number of the children of Israel be as the sand of the sea, a *remnant* shall be saved" (citing Is. 10:20–23). The prophecy of Isaiah declares that "the remnant of Israel. . . shall stay upon the Lord, the Holy One of Israel, in truth. The remnant *shall return*, even the remnant of Jacob unto the mighty God." Through the Apostle Peter we learn that this prophecy was fulfilled in those Israelites who believed

on the Lord Jesus through the preaching of the Gospel.
As he also says, " For ye were as sheep going astray,
but *are now returned* unto the Shepherd and Overseer
of your souls " (1 Pet. 2:25).

Isaiah's prophecy also foretells a "consumption decreed
. . . in righteousness. For the Lord God of hosts shall
make a consumption, even determined, in the midst of
all the land."

This "consumption" "decreed" and "determined," is
spoken of in Rom. 9:28 as the "short work" (*i.e.*, a
matter finished and ended), which the Lord has finished
and "cut short in righteousness." The idea here expressed
is that of an account long held open by the kindness of
the creditor, but at last finally closed, the debtors' credit
being then cut off. This is the long-deferred judgment
of God upon the unbelieving Israelites, in at last cutting
them off from their spiritual privileges, (this corresponds
with the " cutting off " of the natural olive branches),
and in admitting into their place believing Gentiles
(which is the grafting in of the wild-olive branches).
Israel in the flesh has now no standing before God.
Their account has been closed for this age.

The number of Israelites thus cut off is very large in
proportion to the remnant. And this was foretold. For
it has been "as Esaias said before, Except the Lord of
Sabaoth had left us a seed, we had been as Sodoma,
and been made like unto Gomorrha" (Rom. 9:29, citing
Is. 1:9). This shows that the executing of God's judgment cut off all but a very few.

"What shall we say then?" What is the conclusion
of the matter? This, namely, that Gentiles (not "*the*
Gentiles" but certain ones, that is to say, such as believe
the Gospel) which followed not after righteousness, have

attained to righteousness, a righteousness, however, which is that of faith. On the other hand, Israel, which followed after the law of righteousness, hath not attained to a law of righteousness. Wherefore? Because they sought not that righteousness that springs out of faith, but that which comes, as it were, out of works of law. For they stumbled at the Stone of Stumbling, thus fulfilling another prophecy of Isaiah, "And He shall be for a sanctuary (a refuge or asylum) but for a Stone of Stumbling and rock of offence to both the houses of Israel" (Is. 8:14). The citation of this prophecy in Rom. 9:23 combines it with Is. 28:16: "Therefore, thus saith the Lord God, Behold I lay in Zion for a foundation a stone, a tried stone (stone of testing) a precious corner stone, a sure foundation: he *that believeth* shall not make haste."

The Christ of God coming as the meek and lowly Man, the servant of Jehovah, with no form nor comeliness to make Him attractive to the natural eye, not to ascend the throne but to be lifted up on the cross, became " a stone of stumbling " to those Israelites who had not the open eye of faith. The Apostle Peter, referring to the same prophecies, and also to Ps. 118:22, said: "Unto you, therefore, *which believe*, He is precious, but unto them which be disobedient (who do not obey the Gospel-call to repentance and faith) the Stone which the builders disallowed, the same is made the head of the corner, and *a stone of stumbling and rock of offence*, even to them which stumble at the word, being disobedient" (1 Pet. 2:7, 8).

Thus Christ causes a division among the people into two distinct classes. ("So there was a division among the people *because of Him*," John 7:43; 9:16; 10:19). To one class, those who believe, He is "precious"—

a safe "refuge," in Whom is found salvation, rest, peace, joy, and deliverance from the wrath to come. To the other class, those who reject the Gospel, He becomes a stumbling stone, and a rock, not of salvation, but of offence. As Simeon prophesied, "this Child is set for the fall and rising up (not rising *again*) of many in Israel" (Luke 2:34). The two classes are here indicated, namely those who fall upon the stone of stumbling, and those who are lifted up, by faith in Him, into life and light and salvation.

The Lord Himself also in speaking to the Pharisees, referred to the prophecy about the Stone which the builders refused, and further said, "And whosoever shall fall on this stone shall be broken; but on whomsoever it shall fall it will grind him to powder" (Matt. 21:44). The effect of stumbling on that stumbling stone was to be "broken," as the branches of the olive-tree were broken off. But when Christ comes again, it will be as the stone seen by Nebuchadnezzar in his vision, a stone cut out of the mountain without hands, smiting the great image of human government upon its feet, breaking them in pieces, and causing the image itself to become like the chaff of the summer threshingfloor, which the wind carries away. (Dan. 2:41–45.)

CHAPTER X.

"The Word of Faith."
Believing unto Righteousness.

In Romans 10 we have the continuation of the subject taken up in the last part of Chapter 9, namely, the failure of the mass of the Israelites to attain to righteousness, because they sought not the righteousness which is out of faith.

Paul declares that the desire of his heart, and his supplication to God for them, is for their salvation, and he testifies of them that they have a zeal for God, but not according to correct knowledge. For *not knowing God's righteousness*, and seeking to establish their own righteousness, thay have *not submitted* unto the righteousness of God (verses 1-3).

Their not knowing God's righteousness was not the excusable ignorance of those who have not heard of it. God's righteousness imputed to Abraham on the ground of faith was revealed in the Scriptures. So verse 18 asks "Have they not heard? yes, verily." In the word "being ignorant" we have the now familiar anglicized-Greek word "agnostic." This is the term that God applies to one who is ignorant because he has closed his heart to the testimony of God. No man is excusable for not knowing what God has plainly declared in His Word. Those who profess themselves to be " agnostic " are wilfully ignorant. They are " without excuse."

This passage indicates the underlying reason for that sort of ignorance which glories in the name "agnosticism." The unbelieving Israelites did not " *submit themselves* unto the righteousness of God." As is recorded of the Pharisees, they "rejected the counsel of God against themselves" (Luke 7:30). They undertook to establish "their own righteousness," being confident of their ability to do so. They had faith in themselves,—none in the Word of God, which said "there is none righteous, no not one." Had they succeeded in their undertaking, the righteousness thus produced would have been indeed "their own." *They* would have been entitled to the credit of it, not God; and they would have had cause whereof to boast.

On the other hand, the acceptance of God's righteousness, necessitates the humbling of the heart before God. It is the act of one who realizes that he is a sinner, perishing, ungodly, helpless, and without strength to do anything for his own recovery. Such as have learned their true condition by the testimony of God's word, are willing and glad to "submit themselves unto the righteousness of God."

"For Christ is the end of the law for (literally *unto*) righteousness, to every one that believeth." (Ver. 4.)

This is one of the most important verses in Scripture. The law set before the Israelite a task which, if successfully accomplished, would have kept him in a state of righteousness. That was "the end" or object of his course of law-keeping. Thus in Deut. 6:24, 25, Moses says, "And the Lord commanded us to do all these statutes, . . . and it shall be *our righteousness*, if we observe to do all these commandments before the Lord our God, as He hath commanded us."

Thus, had any Israelite trodden the path of the law, without deviation from it all his days, he would have attained and continued in a state of righteousness.

But now, by the Gospel, we have the comforting and most welcome announcement that Christ is Himself the end or object sought by the law (but never attained through the law, because it was weak through the flesh) to *every one that believeth*. This is an explanation of what is said in Isaiah 28:16, quoted in the last verse of Rom. 9, and again in verse 11 of Rom. 10. "*Whosoever believeth* shall not be ashamed" (or put to shame). The word "whosoever" is the same word rendered "every one" in Rom. 10:4. So we may read "*Every one that believeth* on Him shall not be ashamed." Why? Because "Christ is the end of the law unto righteousness to *every one that believeth.*"

This "end" is reached immediately one believes on Him. For the believer becomes at once clothed, by the gift of God's free grace, with a righteousness accomplished by the Son of God on the cross.

On the other hand, the road to righteousness by way of the law was a life-long journey; and the "life" that was its promised reward was not eternal life, which is bestowed on those who have God's righteousness but was merely the continuance of ordinary human life, as Moses said, "that He might preserve us *alive, as at this day*" (Deut. 6:24).

And now we come to a wonderful and illuminating comparison between the word of the law, or what the *law* said to Israelites, in regard to righteousness, and "the word of faith," or what the Gospel says to all men, in regard to righteousness.

Moses describes the righteousness which is of the law

(has law as its source) when he says "that the man which *doeth* those things (the things commanded by the law) shall *live* by them." (See Lev. 18:3; Deut. 6:24.)

The particular passage selected for comparison with the message of the Gospel is Deut. 30:11-14, where Moses says: "For this commandment which I command thee this day is not hidden from thee, neither is it far off,"—for God does not hide His will for man in mystery, nor does He put it out of man's reach. "It is not in heaven that thou shouldst say, Who shall go up for us to heaven and bring it unto us, that we may hear it and *do it?* Neither is it beyond the sea that thou shouldst say, Who shall go over the sea for us, and bring it unto us, that we may hear it, and *do it?* But the word is very nigh unto thee, in thy mouth, and in thy heart, that thou mayest *do it.*"

For the man who was under law everything depended upon *doing* the things commanded. "Life and good" were promised to those who should hear the word of the law "and *do it.*" The words "do it" occur three times in that short passage.

But no man ever attained to righteousness and life by his doing of the law. It was impossible in the state into which man has fallen through sin. "For if there had been a law given which could have given life, verily, righteousness would have been by the law" (Gal. 3:21).

But "the word of faith" speaks in a very different way. The righteousness which is out of faith speaketh on this wise, "Say not in thine heart Who shall ascend into heaven? (that is, to bring Christ down"—for *He* is our righteousness—): Or, who shall descend into the deep? (that is, to bring up Christ again from the dead)." For it is not the *commandment* to be done,

that is now the way to righteousness, but *Christ* to be
believed on. "But what saith it? The word is nigh
thee, in thy mouth, and in thy heart: that is, the word
of faith which we preach; that if thou shalt confess
with thy mouth the Lord Jesus (that is, acknowledge
Jesus as Lord) and believe in thine heart that God
hath raised Him from the dead, thou shalt be saved."
(Verses 6–9.)

The righteousness which is that of faith speaks of
"the word" which is in the mouth and in the heart
of the man who has this righteousness. That word
which thus has its abiding place in the heart and mouth
of man is "the word of faith," which the apostles of
Christ preached. It is not a word of law, bidding men
do the things commanded as the condition of having
righteousness and life. The absence of this word " do"
is a prominent characteristic of the word of faith which
is preached for the salvation of sinners. And the response
that it requires is confession with the mouth that Jesus,
the crucified and risen One, is Lord.

To confess Jesus as Lord is a very different thing
from merely saying with the lips "Lord, Lord" (Matt.
7:22). To confess Him now before men is a great thing
in His eyes; for He said "Whosoever therefore shall
confess Me before men, him will I confess also before
My Father which is in heaven" (Matt. 10:32). To
own him voluntarily as Supreme Lord, in the face of the
world which put Him to a shameful death, is to glorify
God the Father. They who do so will He also own
or acknowledge as His, before His Father in heaven.

In the coming day of His power, *every* tongue shall
confess that Jesus is Lord to the glory of God, the Father
(Phil. 2:11). They will be compelled to do so. But

now the confession of Jesus as Lord is a matter of the
individual will. It must be voluntary. There is no
compulsion.

The confession of Jesus as *Lord* involves the owning
of His absolute authority, and the submission of the
will to Him in entire obedience. The conclusion of
Peter's address to the Jews on Pentecost was in these
words: "Therefore, let all the house of Israel know
assuredly that God hath made *that same Jesus*, whom
ye have crucified, both *Lord* and *Christ*" (Acts 2:36).
As "Christ" He is the anointed One promised of old
and now come into the world as Man to accomplish
all the purposes of God. As "Lord" He is invested with
supreme and absolute authority in heaven and on earth.

Therefore, truly to own Jesus as Lord is to be in full
accord with what God has done in exalting Him to the
highest place. This can only be done through the Holy
Spirit. For the Apostle says: "Wherefore I give you to
understand that . . . no man can say that Jesus is the
Lord, but by the Holy Ghost" (1 Cor. 12:3).

For the confession of Jesus as Lord with the *mouth*
is the result of the work of the Spirit in the *heart*. Particular attention should be given to the way the heart
and mouth are associated in this Scripture. Christ
quoted to the Pharisees the prophecy of Isaiah, saying,
"Ye hypocrites, well did Esaias prophecy of you, saying,
This people draweth nigh unto Me with their *mouth*
and honoureth Me with their *lips*, but their *heart* is far
from Me." (Matt. 15:7, 8; Is. 29:13.)

The "word of faith," however, is not in the mouth
only, but also in the heart. In the mouth it results
in confession of Jesus as Lord. In the heart it produces
faith in Him; so that of the fulness of *heart* the *mouth*

may speak of Him. That which the heart believes of Him through the hearing of faith is "that God hath raised Him from the dead."

The resurrection of Jesus Christ from the dead is the prime fact of the Gospel. Without it there would be no Gospel, no faith, no salvation, no Christ, no Lord. (1 Cor. 15:14-19). Faith rests upon a risen Saviour. Not to know Jesus Christ, the Son of God, as *risen from the dead*, is not to know Him at all. For they who deny or doubt His actual bodily resurrection from among the dead make Him to be still under the power of death like the sinners whom He died to save.

It is not faith to believe in Jesus Christ merely as having come into the world and as having died for sinners. Faith rests securely upon a *living* Saviour. A dead Christ could not save from death. Therefore, the word of faith proclaims a living Christ. If Christ be not risen, then His mission ended in failure, and His death was not death's destruction, but death's complete triumph.

Therefore, the man who knows Jesus Christ in his heart as risen from the dead, and who confesses Him with his mouth as Lord, shall be saved. In that man God has done a work that will never be undone. For "the preparations of the *heart* in man and the answer of the *tongue* is FROM THE LORD" (Prov. 16:1). That man realizes the desire of David when he said, "Let the words of my *mouth* and the meditation of my *heart*, be acceptable in Thy sight, O Lord, my Strength, and my Redeemer" (Ps. 19:14).

"For with the heart man believeth unto righteousness and with the mouth confession is made unto salvation."

"Man *believeth* unto righteousness."

The importance of this statement cannot be over-

estimated. Righteousness is something to which man
must attain in order to be acceptable unto God. There
is then a way whereby sinful man may reach the condition of righteousness. That way is by believing on the
risen Christ, the Son of God. There is no other way.
The only other possible way was by doing the things
commanded by the law. But the trial of 1500 years
under the holy law of God was a demonstration to *man*
(for God did not need the proof) that none could become
righteous by works of law.

"With the *heart* man believeth unto righteousness."

The message of the Gospel is addressed to man's
heart; and until it reaches the heart it is without effect.
Being the message of Infinite Love, announcing that
God has done for the undeserving man what the imagination of man could never have conceived, and at a cost
which the mind of man cannot estimate, it must either
move the heart of man to repentance and faith, or else
leave him harder than before.

"With the heart man believeth."

It is not, as is sometimes suggested, that there is a
difference between believing with the head and believing
with the heart. The fact is that belief is altogether
a matter of the heart, and not of the head. Unless a
man believes with the heart he does not believe at all.
The assent of the intellect to a statement or a creed is
not belief. Faith is a condition of the heart. The Lord
said to His two disciples on the road to Emmaus, "O
foolish men, and slow of *heart* to *believe* all that the
prophets have spoken "(Luke 24:25).

The expression "unto righteousness" in verse 10 throws
light upon the statement of verse 4 that Christ is the end
of the law *unto righteousness* to every one that believeth.

Faith is the attitude of the heart that rests upon the Risen Christ. Thus he that believeth on Him believes *unto righteousness*. That which the law had in view as its "end" or object, Christ *is* to everyone that believes.

It is to be noted that the Scripture always speaks of saving faith in the present tense. "Whosoever believeth," "Every one that believeth." It is never said that whosoever believed, at some past time or other, is saved; though doubtless one who truly believes on Christ continues so to do. The proof that I once believed on the Son of God is that I do so *now*. Without *this* proof, other evidence would be vain. So it is the man that *believes*, that man who *is* (not was) a believer, the man who confesses, the man who calls upon the Lord, that is accepted of God.

In proof that man believeth unto righteousness, the Spirit cites again Is. 28:16, "Whosoever believeth on Him shall not be ashamed." (On the other hand, those who do not believe will wake in eternity "to shame and everlasting contempt," Dan. 12:2; and in proof that with the mouth confession is made unto salvation—that is to say, the confession of Jesus as Lord, is unto the salvation of the one who so confesses Him—the Spirit cites Joel 2:32, "For whosoever shall call upon the Name of the Lord shall be saved."

These proof-texts are broad enough in their terms to embrace Gentiles as well as Jews. Moreover, the character of God's righteousness is such that participation in it could not be a mere matter of natural birth. Accordingly we have the statement that in this vital matter "there is no difference between the Jew and the Greek; for the same Lord over all is rich unto all that call upon Him." (Ver. 12.)

How vastly important then it is that men should call upon the Name of the Lord! Their eternal salvation depends upon it. But, in order that they may call *upon* Him, they must first believe *in* Him; and in order that they may believe in Him, they must first hear *of* Him; and in order that they may hear of Him, there must be a preacher of the Gospel sent unto them—one qualified by God and sent by God on this life-saving mission to his fellow men. (Verses 14, 15.) Therefore, Christ sent His disciples unto all the world and commanded them to preach, in His Name, repentance and the forgiveness of sins, among all nations.

It is a beautiful thing in God's eyes to see the *feet* of His evangelists hastening on this mission. (Ver. 15.) " How beautiful are *the feet* of them that preach the Gospel of peace, and being glad tidings of good things " (quoting Is. 52:7. Cf. Eph. 2:17). God speaks of the *feet* of His gospel-preachers as beautiful. He commends the activity of the feet, rather than the eloquence of the lips. For the state of the sinners is such that the word must be *brought* to them. The evangelists BRING glad tidings of good things. May we seek, therefore, to have our feet shod with the preparation of the Gospel of peace, (Eph. 6:15) being always prepared to carry the message to whomsoever we may be sent. (See Acts 13:26.)

The Gospel of the Risen Christ is "the gospel of *peace*." For "the work of righteousness shall be peace" (Is. 32:17). "Being justified by faith we have peace with God." The word that the risen Lord spake to His disciples when He appeared after His resurrection was "Peace be unto you;" and "He showed them His hands and His feet" (Luke 24:36–40).

"But they (the Israelites) have not all obeyed the

gospel. For Esaias saith, Lord, who hath believed our report?" (Rom. 10:16).

This " report," spoken of by Isaiah (Isa. 53), is the report of the One Who was despised and rejected of men, Who was brought as a lamb to the slaughter, Who was wounded for our trangressions, Who poured out His soul unto death, and to Whom the promise was given " He shall see of the travail of His soul and be satisfied." For the question " Who hath believed our report?" stands at the beginning of the 53rd Chapter of Isaiah. *That is the "report" which produces faith unto righteousness.* As is there written, "By His knowledge shall My Righteous Servant *justify many;* for He shall bear their iniquities" (Is. 53:11).

"So then faith cometh *by the report*, and the report by the Word of God." ("Report" in ver. 16, and "hearing" in ver. 17, are the same word. It is not the act of hearing but the thing heard, the report, that produces faith.)

Did not Israel know this One, by the knowledge of Whom comes righteousness? No. It was foretold that they would not know Him. "He was in the world, and the world was made by Him, and the world knew Him not" (John 1:10). Christ said to them "Ye neither know Me nor My Father" (John 8:19). Paul said, "because they knew Him not" they desired "that He should be slain" (Acts 13:27, 28.)

Moses predicted in his last words that God would move the Israelites to jealousy with those which were not a people, and provoke them to anger with a foolish nation (Deut. 32:21).

To the same effect, but with greater distinctness, Isaiah said, "I was found of them that sought Me not;

I was manifest unto them that asked not after Me" (Is. 65:1). These Scriptures foretell the preaching of the gospel among the Gentiles, who had no knowledge whatever of the true God.

On the other hand, in regard to Israel, Isaiah said in the same passage, "All day long I have stretched forth My hands unto a disobedient and gainsaying people" (Is. 65:2).

This tenth Chapter of Romans, which is of exceeding importance, shows that the righteousness, which the law sought but could not produce, has been accomplished by Christ. (Rom. 10:4, cf. 8:3, 4). It shows that the only way to righteousness and life for perishing sinners is by faith in the risen Christ. It shows that this way of righteousness is available for Gentiles as well as for Jews. And it shows by the Old Testament Scriptures, that many Jews would fail to receive the Gospel, notwithstanding it was "promised afore" to them, and notwithstanding that in fulfilment of God's promise, it was proclaimed first to them.

CHAPTER XI.

The Olive Tree.

(Rom. 11:1-24.)

Did God then cast away the "disobedient and gain-saying people" to whom He vainly stretched out His hands all day long? Many Christians seem to think so. But the answer of Scripture is emphatically that "God hath not cast away His people which He fore-knew."

Paul cites his own wonderful conversion as proof that God had not turned away from His people. Had He done so, Saul of Tarsus would certainly have been allowed to perish in his blind zeal and hatred of Christ.

Furthermore, the Apostle recalls that, even in the darkest days of Israel's apostasy, in the time of Ahab and Jezebel, when Elijah thought that he alone was left of the worshippers of Jehovah, there was nevertheless a faithful remnant of 7000 who had not bowed to Baal.

"Even so, then, *at this present time*," the Apostle declares, "there is a remnant according to the election of grace."

Referring again to Joel 2:32 where occur the words "And it shall come to pass that whosoever shall call on the Name of the Lord shall be delivered," we read there also, "for in Mount Zion and in Jerusalem shall be deliverance, as the Lord hath said, *and in the remnant* whom the Lord shall *call*."

It should be carefully noted that the fulfilment of this prophecy regarding the called remnant of Israel, is expressly said to be "at this present time." This statement demands special notice inasmuch as there are now many who teach that the "Jewish remnant" is a distinct company from the church and belongs to the period of the earthly ministry of the Lord Jesus, or to some fragment of time at the end of this age, after the removal of the church to meet the Lord in the air. The teaching of Scripture, on the contrary, is that the elect remnant is the believing company of Israelites in *this present age*, and that they with the addition of the believing Gentiles, constitute the Church of God. This is also the clear teaching of 1 Pet. 2:4-10, as already pointed out.

The statement of verse 7 of our chapter (Rom. 11) is very explicit: "What then? Israel hath not obtained that which he seeketh for; *but the election hath obtained it,* and the rest were blinded " (or hardened).

What Israel sought after, *i.e.*, righteousness, and all that accompanied it, life, the adoption, the glory, etc.— Israel as a nation hath not obtained. But the election *hath* obtained it. The remnant had already, even in the apostle's day, obtained what God had promised to Israel. Paul declared to the Jews at Antoich in Pisidia, " the glad tidings " namely, " that the promise which was made into the fathers, God *hath fulfilled the same unto us their children* in that He hath raised up Jesus again, as it is written in the Second Psalm " Acts 13:32, 33. The remnant then steps into the place of Israel, and fills that place, receiving all that was promised to Israel in their Messiah.

That the mass of the Israelites would be blinded

was foretold by Isaiah (29:10) and David (Ps. 69:22), which Scriptures are cited. (Verses 8, 9:10.)

However, they have not stumbled that they might fall; but rather that, through their fall, (literally, *offence*), salvation might come to the Gentiles, for to provoke them to jealousy. (Referring again to Deut. 32:21). And now the Apostle looks beyond this age, during which the majority of the Israelites are blinded, saying that if their offence be the riches of the world, and their default the riches of the nations, how much more their fulness? "For," says Paul, "I am speaking to you, Gentiles, inasmuch as I am the Apostle of the Gentiles. I glorify my ministry, if by any means I may provoke to jealousy my own flesh, and may save some from among them." (verses 11, 14).

That is to say, while discharging his ministry as apostle to the Gentiles, Paul had always before him the desire and purpose expressed in the words of Chapter 10:1, "My heart's desire and prayer to God for Israel is that they might be saved." So he strove by provoking them to jealousy (see for example Acts 28:28), to save some from among them now; and he comforted himself with the assurance that, when the predicted period of blindness should be ended, "all Israel shall be saved" (verse 26).

"For if the casting away of them be the reconciling of the world, what shall the receiving of them be but life from the dead. For if the firstfruit be holy, the lump also is holy; and if the root be holy so are the branches" (verses 15, 16).

The reference in the first clause of this verse is to the heave offering of the first of the lump of dough; as written in Numb. 15:21, "Of the first of your dough ye shall give unto the Lord an heave offering."

The remnant of Israel that turned to the Lord, beginning at Pentecost, is regarded as " the first of the dough "
or lump; and as a promise of the future salvation of all
Israel. It is very significant that the Divinely appointed
ceremony for the day of Pentecost called for the offering
of "two wave loaves," which are described as "the
firstfruits unto the Lord" and as "the bread of the firstfruits . . . *holy* to the Lord" (Lev. 23:17-20).

Those two wave-loaves typified the work of God in
this Pentecostal age, that is to say, the gathering of the
firstfruits of the harvest out of Jews and Gentiles.
This gathering or calling out (*ecclesia* or *church*) is the
earnest of the harvest to be gathered in the coming
age, as foretold in Acts 15:14-17. God is now visiting
the Gentiles "to *take out* of them a people for His Name.
And to this agree the words of the prophets, as it is
written, After this I will return, and will build again
the tabernacle of David that is fallen down; . . . that
the residue of men might seek after the Lord, and *all the
Gentiles* upon whom My Name is called, saith the Lord."

This reference to the wave-offering of the day of Pentecost serves also to explain Paul's statement in Rom.
15:15, 16, where he speaks of—"the grace that is given
to me of God, that I should be the minister of Jesus Christ
to the Gentiles, ministering the Gospel of God, that the
offering up of the Gentiles might be acceptable, being sanctified by the Holy Ghost."

Rom. 11:16, second clause, says that if the root be holy
or sanctified, the branches also will be holy.

This introduces the figure of a tree, sanctified or set
apart for God. It points to the fact that the branches
partake of the benefit of the root; and this is true

even of branches that have been graffed in from other trees; for they also partake of the root, having the same share therein as the natural branches.

The illustration of the Olive tree (verses 17–24) is so fully explained in the text of the Scripture itself that its meaning can hardly be missed. We have already referred to the main lesson taught by this illustration, so that it remains but to notice certain interesting and important details.

The illustration is taken from Jer. 11:16 and Ps. 52:8, in connection with which it should be studied.

Jer. 11:16 reads, "The Lord called thy name a green olive tree, fair and of goodly fruit; with the noise of a great tumult He hath kindled a fire upon it and *the branches of it are broken*." This clearly foretold the judgment that was soon to fall upon Israel. It indicates, however, that the overthrow was not to be complete. The tree was not to be uprooted; nor was it to be cut down. Only "the branches" were to be broken off, leaving the root in the ground.

Hosea, whose prophecy is so closely connected with the lesson of Rom. 9-11, says of Israel: "His *branches shall spread*, and his beauty shall be as the *olive tree*" (Hos. 14:6). This shows that the root retains vitality, and shall put forth live branches. It points to the time indicated in Rom. 11:24, when God shall graff the natural branches in again.

In Ps. 52:8, 9, we read, "I am like a green olive tree in the house of God. I trust in the mercy of God for ever and ever. I will praise Thee for ever, because Thou hast done it."

This must refer to Christ; that is to say, to Christ and His members,—the branches, the believing Jews and believing Gentiles, all alike partaking of the root and fatness of the olive tree.

The object which the Apostle to the Gentiles had in view when he so clearly and emphatically taught the relative positions of believing Jews and believing Gentiles in Christ, was to warn the latter against boasting. That there has been, and is, great need of this warning is all too evident. The Church of Christ has come to be generally regarded as a great *Gentile* institution, into which an insignificant number of Jewish " converts " have been brought by means of " missions to the Jews," and in which they are suffered by tolerance. Other Jews are sometimes classed in public religious services with " Turks, infidels, and hereticks." It has been almost wholly forgotten that the Christian Church has been formed by means of *Jewish* missions to *Gentiles*, at the express command of the Risen Lord, given to His Jewish disciples—(Matt. 28:19, 20).

Let us then lay this lesson to heart, and be not high minded, but fear. "For if God spared not the natural branches, take heed lest He also spare not thee. Behold the goodness and severity of God; on them which fell, severity; but toward thee, goodness, if thou continue in His goodness; otherwise thou also shalt be cut off. And they also (Israel), if they abide not still in unbelief, shall be graffed in; for God is able to graff them in again. For if thou wert cut out of the olive tree that is wild by nature and wert graffed, contrary to nature, into a good olive tree; how much more shall these, which be the natural branches, be graffed into their own olive tree?"

No words are needed to elucidate this argument and none could add to its force. By meditating upon it we

may come to realize more clearly the humbling lesson
of God's extraordinary goodness to us, Gentiles by
nature.

The same lesson is taught by the Apostle in his letter
to the Ephesians, to whom he says, "Wherefore remember
that ye being in time past Gentiles in the flesh . . . that
at that time ye were without Christ, being *aliens from
the commonwealth of Israel,* and strangers from the covenants of promise, having no hope, and without God
in the world." " But now," he adds, " in Christ Jesus
ye who sometimes were far off are made nigh by the
blood of Christ. . . Ye are no more strangers and
foreigners, but fellow citizens with the saints (Israelites)
and of the household of God " (Eph. 2:12, 13, 19).

The passage last quoted from Rom. 11:24 also contains
a very clear indication that the day would come when
the period of Gentile privilege in equality with Jews,
would end; and that the Lord would then turn again
to His own people. Surely there are many signs on the
surface of current events that that day is near. Therefore, the gospel message should be pressed all the more
earnestly in the little while that remains.

CHAPTER XII.

The Mystery.

(Rom. 11:25-36.)

We come now to the subject of the "mystery."

"For I would not, brethren, that ye should be ignorant of this mystery, lest ye should be wise in your own conceits; that blindness in part is happened to Israel, until the fulness of the Gentiles be come in."

There is need to look closely at the Scripture before us in order that we may ascertain with certainty what the "mystery" is, whereof the Spirit of God wishes us to be not ignorant.

It is evident from this passage and from other writings of the Apostle Paul, that his ministry had largely to do with a " mystery "; that is to say, with something which lay in the eternal counsels of God, but which He had not made known by the Old Testament Scriptures.

Some of the matters stated in Rom. 11:25 and context were very clearly set forth in the Old Testament. So these cannot constitute the mystery. Paul, however, described his gospel as " the preaching of Jesus Christ, according to the *revelation of the mystery*, which was kept secret since the world began, but now is made manifest by the Scriptures of the prophets (literally, by prophetic writings, meaning the books of the New Testament) according to the commandment of the everlasting God,

made known to *all nations* for the obedience of faith"
(Rom. 16:25, 26).

It was not a thing "kept secret" that blindness should
happen to Israel; for that was clearly stated in Old
Testament Scriptures, and the Apostle himself quotes
them in this very chapter to prove that Israel's present
state of blindness had been distinctly foretold. So
that could not be the mystery.

Neither was it a truth previously hidden, that eventually all Israel was to be saved; for the Apostle quotes,
in proof of that, the words of Isaiah (59:20 and 27:9).

The great mystery of God with which the Apostle Paul
had so much to do did not relate to God's purposes for
Israel, but to His purposes for the Gentiles. It was the
preaching of the Gospel of the grace of God to Gentiles
on a perfect equality with the Jews. It was the announcement to Jew and Gentile alike of precisely the same salvation, on precisely the same terms (the "obedience of
faith"), without any regard whatever to the distinction
that God had previously established between the Israelites
and the Gentiles. Briefly stated, the mystery is just
that which is figured by the illustration of the olive tree,
namely, the admission of Gentiles to an equal share with
Jews in "*their* spiritual things,"—"the root and fatness
of the olive tree."

Paul preached the gospel "according to the revelation
of this mystery, which was kept secret since the world
began, but is now made manifest"; that is to say, he
went forth announcing the glad tidings of God's mercy
through Jesus Christ to both Jew and Gentile alike, in
pursuance of this new revelation of God. The concluding words of Rom. 16:26 make clear what the mystery was. It was the preaching of Jesus Christ, according

to the commandment of the everlasting God, *to all nations* for the obedience of faith.

When the Lord Jesus Christ, after His resurrection, commanded His disciples to preach repentance and the remission of sins in His Name *among all nations* (Gentiles) He commanded them to do that which had not been foretold by the prophets.

Peter obeyed this command, preaching the gospel "according to the revelation of the mystery", when he went to the house of Cornelius (Acts 10); and this was before Paul began his apostolic labours among the Gentiles. For to Peter, first of all, Christ " revealed," through the vision of the great sheet let down from heaven, that Gentiles were to be admitted to all the blessings of the Gospel.

Peter accordingly preached, to Cornelius and his household, " Jesus Christ Who was slain and hanged on a tree, Whom God raised up the third day," and he announced the good tidings that through His Name, whosoever believeth in Him shall receive remission of sins. Thereupon the Gentiles who heard the word received the Holy Spirit, Who is the earnest of the promised inheritance; and were baptized (Acts 10:34-48).

Peter, who first preached the gospel with the Holy Ghost sent down from heaven to an assembled company of Jews, was also the first to preach the same gospel of the remission of sins through faith in the risen Christ to an assembled company of Gentiles. He called this fact to mind at the conference of the apostles and elders at Jerusalem, saying: "Men and brethren, ye know how that a good while ago God *made choice among us*, that the Gentiles by *my* mouth should hear *the word of the Gospel*" (for there is but one gospel) "and believe. And God which knoweth the hearts, bare them witness, giving *them* the Holy Ghost, even as He did unto us; and put *no difference between us and them*, purifying *their* hearts by faith" (Acts 15:7-9).

And it should be noted that Paul does not say that the mystery of Gentile participation in Israel's spiritual things was revealed exclusively or specially to him; but says that "it is now revealed unto His (Christ's) holy *apostles and prophets* by the Spirit, that the Gentiles should be fellow heirs," etc. (Eph. 3:5, 6).

We thus see that the same gospel is for the Gentiles and for the Jews; and that those who believe it, whether Jews or Gentiles, are admitted into precisely the same privileges and blessings. The believing ones, whether Jews or Gentiles, become "living stones", and are forthwith placed in the great house that God is building upon Christ, the true Foundation. (1 Cor. 3:10, 11; 1 Pet. 2:4-0.)

We conclude, therefore, that the "mystery" mentioned in Romans 11 is nothing more nor less than that new revelation of God's counsels, which the inspired Apostle has been setting forth in this Epistle, namely that, between the predicted breaking off of the branches of the olive tree, and the predicted time when all Israel shall be saved, there was determined, in the previously hidden counsels of God, an era during which there should be a great ingathering of believing Gentiles, and that these should become, equally with believing Israelites, partakers of the promises of God in Christ.

In Rom. 11:25 the words that specially refer to the mystery are these: "until the fulness of the Gentiles be come in." When the fulness, or complete number

of Gentile believers, shall have "come in" to the place
now offered to them among the natural branches of the
good olive tree, then the blindness now lying upon the
hearts of the mass of the Israelites shall be removed.
As is also stated in 2 Cor. 3:15, 16: "But even unto
this day, when Moses is read, the veil is upon their
heart. Nevertheless when it shall turn to the Lord,
the veil shall be taken away."

So then, the "mystery" here referred to is not that the
blindness now resting upon the Israelites is to be removed,
but that there is to be first a great ingathering of Gentiles
in response to the preaching of the Gospel in all the
world.

We have already seen that the Epistle to the Ephesians
presents many points of resemblance to that section of
Romans which is now before us. There we read of the
"adoption" as being in the eternal counsels of God
and as embracing both Jews and Gentiles; of redemption through the blood of Christ, the remission of sins;
of the purpose of God, which He purposed in Himself;
of the predestined inheritance of the children of God;
and of the Holy Spirit of promise, who is the earnest
of our inheritance until the redemption of the purchased
possession, unto the praise of His glory (Eph. 1:3–14).

In those verses the identical gospel, set forth more
amply in Romans, is distinctly declared.

Moreover, in Eph. 1:9 Paul mentions that God has
"made known unto us the mystery of His will," that
is to say, that part of God's eternal purpose which He
had not previously revealed. And in Chapter 3, the
inspired writer proceeds to state what that mystery
is, saying that "by revelation He made known unto
me the mystery" (the language is similar to that of

Rom. 16:25) "which in other ages was not made known
unto the sons of men, as it is now revealed unto His
holy apostles and prophets (writers of the 'prophetic
scriptures' of the N. T.) by the Spirit." Then follows
a statement of the mystery, given in a few simple and
clear words: "That the Gentiles should be fellow heirs,
and of the same body, and partakers of His promise in
Christ, by (means of) the Gospel, whereof I was made
a minister." (Eph. 3:5-7.)

Here again the mystery is declared to be the equal
participation of Gentiles with Jews in that which was
supposed, from the Old Testament prophecies, to be
the exclusive privilege of the Jews. Literally the words
are " that the Gentiles should be joint-heirs, of a joint-
body, and joint-partakers of His promise in the Christ."

That "joint-body" is, of course, the church, the Body
of Christ which is now being gathered out from all
nations.

The Epistle to the Ephesians makes it particularly
clear that the church is primarily Jewish, and that the
place of the Gentile therein is a matter of special grace
now extended to them, and not covenanted in the Old
Testament Scriptures. In Chapter 2, the Gentile saints
are exhorted to remember that in time past they were
" without Christ, being aliens from *the commonwealth
of Israel*, and strangers from the covenants of promise,
having no hope, and without God in the world " (verse
12). But the revelation of the mystery changes completely their status. They who once were " far off "
are now " made nigh by the blood of Christ " (verse 13).
They are no longer " strangers and foreigners, but fellow-
citizens with the saints (the Israelites, see Deut. 33:3,

27–29), and of the household of God, and are being built (together with the believing Israelites) upon the foundation of the apostles and prophets, Jesus Christ Himself being the chief corner-stone."

In other words, the Jewish privileges, promises and covenants, everything in fact that was secured to them by the Word of God in Christ, remain unchanged, for God's gifts and calling are without change of purpose on His part. Those who are true Israelites come into all these blessings. The coming of Christ did not alter the status of the Israelites in respect to the promises of God. But the difference with respect to the Gentiles is immense. From being "without Christ, aliens from the commonwealth of Israel," they are made, by the grace of God, fellow-citizens with the saints, and joint-partakers with them in His promise in Christ.

Paul tells us that this hitherto hidden purpose of God is now being accomplished *by means of the Gospel*, whereof he was made a minister; and in explanation of this he further says: "unto me, who am less than the least of all saints, is this grace given, that I should preach *among the Gentiles* the unsearchable riches of Christ" (Eph. 3:8).

The unsearchable riches of Christ are the spiritual blessings wherewith God has blessed us in Christ (Eph. 1:3). They are those good things passing man's understanding, which God has prepared for them that love Him (1 Cor. 2:9). The announcing of those riches of Christ *to the Gentiles*, who were "without Christ," is the preaching of the gospel according to the revelation of the mystery.

Further reference to this mystery is found in Colossians. Paul again in that Epistle refers to "the hope of the

Gospel, which was preached to every creature which is under heaven, of which I, Paul, am made a minister" (1:23); and he speaks of the Body of Christ, the church, whereof also he was made a minister "to fulfil the Word of God, *the mystery* which hath been hidden from ages and from generations, but now is made manifest to His saints, to whom God would make known what is the riches of the glory of *this mystery among the Gentiles*, which is, Christ in *you* (Gentiles) the *hope of glory*, Whom we preach " (Col. 1:25–28).

From this again it is clear that the mystery now revealed, and in accordance with which the Gospel is now being preached, is the presentation of Christ in all His fulness to the Gentiles. We have the words "this mystery *among* the Gentiles which is Christ *in* you (Gentiles) the hope of glory." The preposition rendered "*among* the Gentiles" is the same as that rendered "*in you*." It would seem that the rendering should be "among" in both places. For it is evident that the point of the passage is the extraordinary fact that Christ is now preached among the Gentiles as "the hope of glory"; whereas the Gentiles theretofore had had "no hope" and no part in Christ, and no prospect of "glory".

Once again Paul refers to the mystery in whose proclamation he had so prominent a part. In 1 Tim. 3:16 he says: " And without controversy great is the mystery of godliness: God was manifest in the flesh, justified in the Spirit, seen of angels, preached unto the Gentiles, believed on in the world, received up into glory."

This is the most comprehensive of all the statements of the mystery. It embraces the incarnation, the work of Christ (things announced by the Gospel and which

the angels desire to look into, 1 Pet. 1:12) and the receiving up of Christ "in glory". But the heart of the mystery
is that Christ, the special hope and expectation of Israel,
was "preached unto *the Gentiles*" and "believed on *in
the world*."

It should be noted that Paul speaks of the revelation
of the mystery, which was committed to him, as that
which fulfils the Word of God (Col. 1:25, 26). That
which gives completeness and finality to the revelation
which God has given to His human creatures, is the
announcement of this wonderful plan, long hidden in
His own heart, to beget to Himself, "by means of
the Gospel" (1 Cor. 4:15) a family of sons, called
out of *all the nations of the world*, to share the glories
prepared for His own Son, Who offered up Himself,
a sacrifice for sin, for the accomplishment of this great
purpose.

Returning now to the concluding verses of Rom. 11,
we find a final reference to the nature of God's present
dealings with His people, Israel. "As touching the
Gospel they are enemies," says Paul, "for your sake";
for the Gentiles are now profiting by the defection of
Israel, as has been already shown. "But as touching
the election, they are beloved for the fathers' sake. For
not to be repented of are the gifts and calling of God."
By this we understand that, although the mass of Israel
has turned away from God their Saviour, there are some
whom God has called (the election, or calling) and who
are beloved for their fathers' sake. An example of
this principle is seen in the fact that for David's sake
God did not take away the entire kingdom from
Rehoboam.

This passage speaks not only of the *gifts* of God, as

the gift of eternal life, the gift of the Spirit, etc., but also of the "calling" of God. That also pertained to Israel, and so Israelites receive it.

"For as ye also in time past were disobedient to God" (the verb here is "were disobedient," not as in the A. V. "have not believed"), " but now have been shown mercy through their disobedience; so also these now were disobedient, to your mercy, that they also may have mercy shown them. For God shut up all together in disobedience, that He might show mercy to all" (verses 28–32 *lit. Gr.*).

Here ends the revelation of the great purpose of God for those whom He has made the objects of His mercy and grace, and of the manner in which that purpose is being accomplished by Him Who is great in counsel and mighty in work, and Who worketh all things after the counsel of His own will.

In contemplation of the purpose of God, and His method of working, now fully set forth, the Apostle bursts into a glowing tribute of wonder and praise.

"O the depth of the riches, both of the wisdom and knowledge of God! How unsearchable are His judgments, and His ways past finding out." None can possibly comprehend the ways of God, except they be shown him by God Himself; for His ways are not as our ways.

"For who hath known the mind of the Lord, and who hath been His counsellor?" With whom shall the Lord take counsel, or who shall be able to advise Him how best to carry out His purposes?

This recalls the words of Isaiah 40:13, 14, which doubtless have reference to the work of this age based on redemption,—"Who hath directed the Spirit of the Lord, or being His counsellor hath taught Him? With whom took He counsel, and who instructed Him, and taught Him in the path of judgment, and showed to Him the way of understanding?"

And finally the Apostle asks:

"Or who hath first given to Him, and it shall be recompensed unto him again?"

This final question seems to direct our attention to the fact that all that is involved in the purpose of God, which is the subject of these Scriptures, is wholly of *grace*. None has *given* anything whatever to God for which he receives as a recompense the place of a son to God. The carrying out of that eternal purpose will be wholly "to the praise of the glory of His *grace*" (Eph. 1:5, 6). We need not look at ourselves and ask: "What did God see in us to impel Him to make us His vessels of mercy?" He saw in us no reason whatever for so doing; but on the contrary, every reason why we should be left to the consequences of our own sins.

"For of HIM, and through HIM, and unto HIM are all things."

What prompted redemption was the love of God. (Is. 63:9; Eph. 1:5–7.) So the originating motive was "of Him." It was, moreover, planned by His infinite wisdom, and accomplished by His mighty power, so that it was "through Him." And not only so, but the results are all "unto Him;" for He has redeemed us and the lost inheritance, unto *Himself*.

"To Whom be glory, for ever. Amen."

CHAPTER XIII.

The "Reasonable Service" of God's Children. The Heavenly Pattern.

We have now traversed the inspired exposition of the Gospel of God given through His servant Paul. We have meditated upon the wonderful revelation of the grace of God displayed in the redemption and justification of sinners, and in calling them into the relationship of sons to Himself.

Our attention must now be directed to what God desires *from* us, in view of all that He has done *for* us. If the revelation of His great love wherewith He loved us even when we were dead in sins has made any impression upon our hearts, there will be awakened in us the desire to make that response for which He is looking. Let us then set ourselves, with purpose of heart, to grasp the lessons of the concluding chapters of Romans. This will require an effort of our wills, because we find it far easier and more agreeable to fill our minds with interesting Biblical facts, than to apply ourselves to the precepts of Scripture, and to conform our walk, and ways, and speech thereto. Nevertheless, it is in these simple, homely precepts that we find the expression of the Father's will for His children; and it is of little avail to know

the outlines of His vast plan of the ages, if we neglect
the least of His commandments.

Romans 12 begins with a very remarkable exhortation: "I beseech you therefore, brethren, by the mercies
of God, that ye present your bodies a living sacrifice,
holy, acceptable unto God, which is your reasonable service. And be not conformed to this world (age); but
be ye transformed by the renewing of your mind, that
ye may prove what is that good, and acceptable, and
perfect will of God."

This exhortation has two parts, one relating to the
body, and the other to the mind. We are besought *first*,
to present our bodies as living sacrifices to God; and
second, to be not conformed to this present age, but to
be transformed by the renewing of our minds. And the
promised result is that we shall "prove," that is, we
shall know by experience, what is the will of God, that
it is good, well pleasing, and perfect.

The exhortation is connected with what has gone before
by the word "therefore." It is because of the revelation of God's purpose for us that we are exhorted to
present our bodies to Him. Moreover, it is based directly upon the "mercies" or compassions of God. All
that God has done and purposes doing for the objects
of His grace, are "mercies." It is all, from first to last,
the carrying out of His purpose revealed when man had
forfeited every claim upon His goodness. Then it was
that God said, " I will have mercy on whom I will have
mercy, and I will have compassion on whom I will have
compassion." (Rom. 9:15.) By these mercies we are
exhorted.

We should also notice the intensity of the desire expressed by the word "beseech." What marvellous grace

is manifested in God thus approaching His creature to beseech him do that which is for the creature's own welfare! We find the same strong expression in other Scriptures. Thus, in 2 Cor. 5:20 we read: "Now then we are ambassadors for Christ, as though God did beseech you by us, we pray you in Christ's stead be ye reconciled to God." In vain would the work of reconciliation have been effected if responsible man should refuse to accept its results, and should choose to continue in enmity against God.

Also in Ephesians, after the revelation of the calling of Jews and Gentiles into one body, Paul says "I *therefore* beseech you that ye walk worthy of the vocation wherewith ye are called, with all lowliness and meekness, with long suffering, forbearing one another, in love endeavoring to keep the unity of the Spirit in the bond of peace." (Eph. 4:1-3.)

It is clear that very much depends—far more than we can realize—upon the heed which we pay to these earnest entreaties of the Spirit of God. Evidently our *bodies* and *minds* are important instruments for the service of God in the carrying out of His purposes for us. Our bodies are His by every right. Yet having given us the use of them, and the responsibility for them, He will not take possession of them unless "presented" to Him.

God will not accept an offering from His people except it be given willingly with the heart. "Speak unto the children of Israel that they bring Me an offering: of every man that giveth it *willingly with his heart* ye shall take My offering " (Ex. 25:2; see Ex. 35:5).

Chap. 11:35 puts the question "Who hath *first* given to Him and it shall be recompensed unto Him again?" Surely none. But now, *after* the riches of God's grace have been bestowed upon us, it is at once made known that there *is* something that we can present to God, namely our bodies. And of course, if we can present them to Him, it is equally in our power to withhold them from Him. Clearly this is a serious matter.

We are told to present our bodies as a "sacrifice." There are two characteristics of a sacrifice or offering to God that should be noticed in this connection. *First*, the sacrifice must be *freely offered*. "He shall offer it of his *own voluntary will* at the door of the tabernacle of the congregation before the Lord" (Lev. 1:3). God will not accept anything that is not offered of the free-will of the offerer. *Secondly*, the offering must be absolute and final. The offerer reserves to himself no part of the thing offered, nor can he ever recall it. Without these conditions the act would not be a sacrifice. So we need to consider this matter carefully, that we deceive not ourselves into thinking that we have presented our bodies to God when we have really reserved them for our own use.

Our bodies are to be *living* sacrifices, not *dying* sacrifices, such as the Israelites offered; for they are to be used in the service of God. God has need of the physical bodies of His people for the carrying on of His work in this present age, both the work of the Gospel, and the manifold ministries of the saints, one to another. Indeed this willing surrender of our bodies to God is declared to be our "reasonable service." That is to say, it is the reasonable, or literally the "logical" thing for us to do, in view of the relationship into which God has brought us to Himself, to the Lord Jesus Christ, and to one another.

This relationship of the saints one to another " in

Christ " is similar to that of the many members forming
one human body. " For as we have many members
in one body, and all members have not the same office;
so we, being many, are one body in Christ, and every one
members, one of another (Ver. 4. 5).

All of the various offices of the many members of this
body " in Christ " must be performed through the
instrumentality of the physical members of the individual
saints who compose that body. This is truth which
it is *worse* than useless for us to know unless we put
it into actual practice.

Much is made, and rightly, of "the truth of the one
body." But must it not be owned with sorrow that
many of those who make much of this truth in speaking
and writing, pay little attention to the essential matter
of habitually *practicing* it? There is great need that
we should examine ourselves before the Lord as to this
matter. It is one in which the *individual will of each
saint must act*. Each one must, for himself, present
his own body for the service of God.

In this, as in everything else that is required of us,
the Lord Jesus is the perfect pattern. He has left us
an example that we should follow in His steps (1 Pet.
2:21). We read that when He came into the world
He said "Sacrifice and offering Thou wouldest not, but
a body hast Thou prepared Me. . . . Then said I, Lo,
I come to do Thy will, O God" (Heb. 10:5, 7). That
body of His flesh prepared for Him was, indeed, offered
up as a *dying* sacrifice, whereas we are besought to present our bodies as *living* sacrifices. But His body was,
all His days, a living sacrifice, wholly given up to do
the will of God. That was His meat and drink (John
4:34). His first recorded utterance shows that His

Father's business occupied all His heart (Luke 2:49); and the whole record of His life reveals the truth of His own saying: "For I came down from Heaven, not to do Mine own will, but the will of Him that sent Me" (John 6:38).

But where, we might ask, is the power whereby we shall be able to carry out this exhortation? We are, by nature, the slaves of our own wills,—the will of the flesh. How then shall we escape from the old habits and ways that were formed in that bondage? The answer is that we are to do this "through the Spirit." Only through the Spirit can anything be done that is acceptable unto God. It is "the law of the Spirit of Life in Christ Jesus" that sets us free from "the law of sin and death." It is "through the Spirit" that we must put to death the deeds of the body (Rom. 8:13). It is " through the Spirit " that we can wait patiently for the hope of righteousness by faith (Gal. 5:5). For it is the Spirit that "helpeth our infirmities." It was "through the Eternal Spirit" that our Lord *"presented Himself* without spot unto God." (Heb. 9:14.)

So, in order to comply with this exhortation, there seems to be needed a real, presonal transaction between our heart and God, whereby we consciously and willingly part with the ownership of our body, withdrawing it from the service of self, and placing it at God's disposal. And then there must be a dependance upon the Spirit of God for power to regard the body and its members as henceforth God's property. Surely when God bids us do a thing, He will supply the power to do it.

Furthermore, we are not to be conformed to this age; that is to say, not formed or moulded according to the pattern of this age. A form, or pattern, is used for the purpose of shaping or moulding things into the likeness or configuration of itself. This age has its patterns, to which those who belong to the age must conform themselves. This is a process of the *mind*. According to the pattern of this age each man should be high-minded, having a good opinion of man in general, and himself in particular. The man whose mind is formed by the principles of this age seeks for himself the highest attainable place in it, pursues steadily his own interest and advantage, expending his thought and effort upon securing for himself some distinction among his fellow men, and the largest possible portion of the honours, wealth, and pleasures of life.

The child of God is exhorted to be *just the reverse* of this, to be, in fact "transformed" by the renewing of his mind.

The two patterns, that of this age, and that given by the Father for His children to follow, are indicated by the Lord's words to His disciples, found in Luke 22:24-26. "And there was also a strife among them, which should be accounted the greatest. And He said unto them, The kings of the Gentiles exercise lordship over them; and they that exercise authority upon them are called benefactors." Here is the pattern of this age, to which we are not to be conformed. "But *ye shall not be so:* but he that is greatest *among you*, let him be as the younger; and he that is chief, as he *that doth serve*."

And furthermore He directs attention to Himself as the Pattern for us, saying, "I am among you as He that *serveth*." As is also written of Him in another Scripture: "He made Himself of no reputation, and took upon Him the *form of a servant* (bondman), and

being found in fashion as a man He *humbled Himself*"
(Phil. 2:7, 8).

In a word, the difference between the pattern of this
age, and the pattern which God sets before us by precept
and by the example of the Lord Jesus, is that between
striving for the highest place, and purposely choosing
the lowest. The world's way is to get ahead of others.
The way of Christ is to put others ahead of self. We
may not dwell upon this matter; but would urge the
reader to note carefully what the Scriptures say as to
importance in God's sight of lowly-mindedness, and true
humility of spirit and heart, manifested in seeking the
lowliest places, and he will be impressed by the fact that
there is nothing of greater practical importance for
the child of God than to humble himself continually
under the mighty hand of God.

Because of what the world has become by reason of
the pride of man and the haughtiness of man's spirit,
there was but one place in it that was possible for the
Son of God to occupy, and that place was the very lowest. Let us remember then that the servant is not
above his Lord, nor the disciple above his Master.

In addition to the change in the *character* of our minds
from haughtiness to lowliness of mind, there should be
also a complete change in the subject of our thoughts.
Thoughts of earthly and temporal things should be
replaced by thoughts of heavenly and eternal things.
Thoughts about our own affairs, desires, expectations,
grievances, disappointments, etc., should give place
to thoughts about "those things which concern the Lord
Jesus Christ." The Apostle's injunction should be
remembered: "Whatsoever things are true, whatsoever
things are honest, whatsoever things are just, whatso-

ever things are pure, whatsoever things are lovely, whatsoever things are of good report, think on *these* things"
(Phil. 4:8).

The promised result of presenting our bodies unto
God, and being transformed by the renewing of our
minds, is that we shall prove what is that good, and
well-pleasing, and perfect will of God.

Our bodies and minds have heretofore been in the
service of self. It has been a hard and degrading service; and those parts of our beings have suffered in
it. We have known nothing of the blessedness of the
will of God while we were in that bondage; but have
reaped the fruits of our own wills, which are not good,
well-pleasing and perfect, but are bad, ill-pleasing and
imperfect. The minds of men have been the abode of
vile, impure, vain and foolish thoughts, and the hatching
place of every scheme of wickedness. Their bodies have
been the agents of every criminal and evil deed. But in
the " reasonable service " of God all that is to be changed.
We may have the single eye, the body full of light, the
ear nailed to wisdom's doorpost, the lips touched with
coals of fire from God's altar, the clean hands washed
in innocency, and the feet shod with the preparation
of the Gospel of peace. O, that it may be the experience
of every one of us to prove the result of presenting our
bodies to God, and of being transformed by the renewing
of our minds!

The remainder of the 12th Chapter of Romans gives
details of God's pattern. They need no comment; but
they do demand our careful attention and implicit obedience. The character of the mind is referred to again
in verse 3, where we are admonished not to think more
highly of ourselves than we ought to think; and in

verse 16, which reads "Be of the same mind one toward another. Mind not high things." Do not set your mind on them. "But condescend to (or rather *associate with*) men of low estate."

This pattern is, indeed, radically different from the pattern of the present age; for it is a heavenly pattern, exhibited in its perfection in the Second Man, Who is " the Lord from heaven." The last verses of the chapter tell how we should treat our enemies, showing kindness to them, giving them food and drink when they are hungry and thirsty, and thus overcoming evil with good. In this feature, as in many others, we note the resemblance to the Lord's own teaching, given to the children of God in what is called the Sermon on the Mount, in which we have, from the Lord's own lips, what may well be regarded as mountain-top teaching indeed: "I say unto you, Love your enemies, bless them that curse you, do good to them that hate you, and pray for them which despitefully use you and persecute you; that *ye may be the children of your Father which is in heaven.*" This is the pattern to which God would have His children conformed. And it goes even further, "Be ye therefore perfect, even as your Father which is in heaven is perfect" (Matt. 5:44, 48).

What then will God have of us? *Perfect conformity to a perfect pattern.* This truly is the very pinnacle of doctrine.

The occupations which God finds for our bodies and minds are first of all in service to our fellow-saints, according as each one has received the gift of God's grace, in prophesying, ministering, teaching, exhorting, giving, overseeing, showing mercy, distributing to the necessity of saints, showing sympathy, using hospitality and so on. (See also 1 Pet. 4:10, 11.)

There are many lines of activity in which God would have us engage; for there is no lack of suitable occupation for the children of God. But the emphasis is laid upon *love*. "Let love be without dissimulation." Let there be *real* love, not a mere pretense. "Be kindly affectioned one to another with brotherly love; in honour preferring one another."

Similar instruction is found in 1 Peter 4:8–11.

CHAPTER XIV.

More Details of the Heavenly Pattern.

(Rom. 13.)

Romans 13:1-7 deals with the subject of the State defining with precision the relation of the children of God thereto. Every soul is to be subject to the higher powers, that is to say, authorities that are placed above him. And the important fact is here stated that no authority exists except it be from God. The powers that be,—the existing authorities—are ordained or appointed of God. Though the government be in the hands of evil and unjust persons, who fear not God neither regard man, nevertheless we are to remember that the *power they exercise* is derived from God. Therefore the authorities should be respected. All resistance to them, whether "passive" or otherwise, is forbidden. For "whosoever resisteth the power, resisteth the ordinance of God; and they that resist shall receive to themselves judgment."

The prophet Daniel said to Nebuchadnezzar, "Thou, O king, art a king of kings: for the *God of heaven* hath *given thee a kingdom, power*, and *strength* and *glory*." (Dan. 2:37.) Nebuchadnezzar's power came from God.

The power which Pilate exercised in sending the Lord Jesus to the cross was given to him "from above." As

Christ said to him, "Thou couldest have no power at all against Me, except it were *given thee from above*" (John 19:11).

The principle involved is that *government is a divine institution*. God is a God of law and order. Lawlessness is the state of those who are not subject to God. "Sin is lawlessness" (1 John 3:4). Therefore, we are to regard with respect even the poor remnants of governmental authority that yet remain to curb the tendencies of men towards lawlessness. Poor and ineffectual as they are, nevertheless they preserve the world from chaos, and make it possible for society to continue. And God does Himself use the machinery of human governments, as is evident from the fact that, through their instrumentality, crimes, particularly murders, are so often brought to light in ways that are remarkable, and their perpetrators punished.

We should therefore be thankful that God's restraining hand has not been wholly withdrawn, and that men are not left wholly free to follow the lawless impulses of their own hearts.

This suggests what will be the eternal state of those who reject the mercy of God. Nothing worse could happen to human beings than that *God should withdraw Himself from them, and leave them to themselves*. If men should be left to a state of utter lawlessness, and free to vent the hatred and malice of their hearts, the resulting torments would be beyond the power of the imagination to conceive. God has not yet withdrawn Himself from the men who are in the world. His sun still shines upon the evil and the good alike.

In like manner God is still represented in the world by government, which calls the evil-doer to account.

Rulers are not a terror to good works, but to evil. The ruler does not in vain bear the sword, which is the symbol of authority to punish wrong-doing. For he is the minister of God, a revenger to execute wrath upon him that doeth evil. Wherefore, we must needs be subject to the constituted authorities, not only because of fear of their wrath, *but also for conscience sake* (verses 4, 5).

For this reason we are commanded to pay tribute (taxes) also. Because the authorities are God's ministers, attending continually upon the matter of maintaining government. "Render, therefore, to all their dues: tribute to whom tribute is due; custom to whom custom; fear to whom fear; honour to whom honour."

The teaching of these verses is but an expansion of the Lord's own command to "Render unto Caesar the things that are Caesar's" (Matt. 22:21).

We have seen how closely the teaching of Peter coincides with that of Paul. On this point also there is perfect agreement. The Apostle Peter says: "Submit yourselves to every ordinance of man *for the Lord's sake:* whether it be to the king as supreme; or unto governors, as unto them that are sent by him for the punishment of evil-doers, and for the praise of them that do well. *For so is the will of God;* that with well-doing ye may put to silence the ignorance of foolish men. As free, and not using your liberty for a cloke of maliciousness, but as the servants of God. Honour all men. Love the brotherhood. Fear God. Honour the King" (1 Pet. 2:13–17).

In a case, however, where human authority commands something to be done which is contrary to the express command of God, then the Christian must refuse

to obey the human authority. Obedience is rendered
to the human authority simply because it is God's command; and, of course, God does not command His people
to disobey His own commands. Thus the three young
Hebrews in Babylon were right in refusing at the decree
of the king to disobey the commandment of Jehovah:
" Thou shalt not make unto thee any graven image. . .
Thou shalt not bow down to them nor serve them."

Also the apostles, whom Christ had commanded to
preach *in His Name*, beginning at Jerusalem, refused to
obey the temple-authorities, when "they called them,
and commanded them not to speak at all, nor teach
in the Name of Jesus. But Peter and John answered
and said unto them, Whether it be right in the sight of
God to hearken unto you more than unto God, judge
ye. For we cannot but speak the things which we have
seen and heard " (Acts 4:18, 19).

The Scriptures manifestly do not contemplate that
Christians should take any part in the management of
the affairs of this world, either by holding office, or
by participating in the choice of officials. The Christian
calling is to a place quite apart from the world. It
makes him a stranger and a pilgrim here. His citizen-
ship (*politeuma*) is in heaven (Phil. 3:20). He represents, in the world, a foreign government, "the Kingdom
of God," being an "ambassador for Christ." That also
requires him to keep absolutely aloof from the politics
of the world. One cannot take the oath of office to
serve an earthly state without disregarding his allegiance
to the Kingdom of God's Son. "The kings of the
earth set themselves, and the rulers take counsel together
against the Lord, and *against* His Christ" (Ps. 2:2);
never *for* Him. Therefore, the man who has submitted

to the authority of the Lord of glory, Whom the rulers of this world crucified (1 Cor. 2:8) could not consistently take office under the rulers of this age; for by so doing he would be associating himself with that which is in principle opposed to Christ.

Christians should make intercession and give thanks for kings, and for all that are in authority; but the object is "that we may lead a quiet and peaceable life, in all godliness and honesty." (1 Tim. 2:1, 2).

Believers are commanded to "owe no man anything" (Rom. 13:8). This should not be taken as limited to money-debts. The meaning seems to be not to leave any obligation undischarged. Whatever we "ought" (*i.e., owe it* to another) to do, we are bidden to do. The words " Owe no man anything " follow immediately after the command to render to all their dues, to pay taxes, etc. So we may take the meaning to be that a Christian is to discharge all his lawful obligations.

But there is one obligation which we can never fully discharge, and that is the debt of love we owe one to another. Here is an instance of the " simplicity that is in Christ." The law given on Sinai and written on two tables of stone consisted of ten commandments, or "ten *Words*." The law of Christ, which the Spirit writes upon the hearts of God's children, consists in *"one* Word." (Gal. 5, 14). The one who obeys the law of love needs not the commandments not to kill, to steal, and to slander, etc. "Love worketh no ill to his neighbour: Therefore love is the fulfilling of the law" (Rom. 13:8-10).

But not only are we to walk in *love*; we are also, as children of God, to walk in *light*. For God is light, as well as love. So the Apostle adds these arousing words:

"And that (lit. *also this*), knowing the time, that now it is high time to awake out of sleep. For us the night is nearly gone. The dawn is so near that, if we would have the day find us not sleeping, we should even now be rousing ourselves out of sleep. As John says: "The darkness is passing away, and the true light is already shining" (1 John 2:8, Gr.).

The salvation for which we are waiting in hope is rapidly approaching. It is "nearer than when we believed." The night of this age, which is enveloped in dense spiritual darkness consequent upon the rejection of the True Light, is far spent. The *day*, in which everything will come to light and its true nature be revealed, is *at hand*. Let us, therefore, cast off all works of darkness, including everything that is in conformity with the doings of this age, and let us put on the armour of light. (See 1 Thess. 5:5-8.) Let us walk *becomingly*, just as we would do if the full glare of the sunlight were shining upon us. Be not engaged in anything which the darkness is relied upon to cover. "But put ye on the Lord Jesus Christ, and make not provision for the flesh to fulfill the lusts thereof."

Similar teaching and exhortation are found in 1 Pet. 4:1-8. Christ has suffered for us in the flesh. We should therefore equip ourselves with the "same mind" that was in Him, not living the rest of our time to the desires of men, but to *the Will of God*. Peter refers also to those who walk in lasciviousness, lusts, excess of wine, revellings, banquetings, etc., and bids us not to have part with them. This exhortation is made very impressive by the words "But the end of all things is *at hand*" (compare Paul's words, "the night is far spent, the day is *at hand*"); "be ye therefore sober, and watch unto prayer.

But *above all* have fervent love among yourselves; for love shall cover the multitude of sins."

Likewise in Ephesians 5 we find the admonition to walk in *love,* followed by that to walk in *light.* "Be ye therefore followers of God as dear (beloved) children. And walk *in love,* as Christ also hath loved us and given Himself for us" (Ver. 1, 2). Then, after a reference to the things which we are to lay aside as having no place in the kingdom of Christ, we read: "For ye were sometimes darkness, but now are ye light in the Lord: walk as *children of light. . . .* and have no fellowship with the unfruitful works of darkness" (Ver. 8–11).

The frequent repetition of these admonitions as to our behaviour testifies to their great importance in the sight of God; and they sharply rebuke the disposition that is in us to give much attention to Scriptures which add to our knowledge of truth, and little to those which contain directions for our daily walk.

Christianity is not merely a system of truth to be believed. It is a life to be lived on earth after the heavenly pattern given in the teachings of the Lord Jesus Christ and His Apostles.

CHAPTER XV.

Receiving the Brethren. Toleration. Judging, etc.

(Rom. 14.)

Chapter 14 of Romans contains admonitions to which we should pay earnest heed; for the neglect of them gives rise to that very distressing evil which abounds at the present day, namely, divisions and strife among brethren.

Most frequently such discords have their origin in some difference of opinion as to matters pertaining to Christian doctrine or practice. This chapter recognizes that there would be divergencies of that sort. Individuals differ in many ways. In fact, no two are alike. This diversity and individuality characterize all the works of God, displaying His manifold wisdom. But this individuality among brethren creates a need for *toleration*. Indeed, forbearance becomes an absolute necessity; and doubtless one purpose of this great diversity is to teach us to practice toleration, and to abstain from judging one another. It is natural to us to think highly of our own opinions and ways; and it follows that we are eager to press them upon others for their acceptance. In fact, the expression by another of opposing views sometimes produces irritation and anger;

and the discussion of such differences frequently engenders strife and estrangement.

As an illustration of divergencies of view that may provoke strife and division, the Apostle instances the question of eating or not eating certain things. The matter of eating meats that had been offered to idols also came into discussion among the saints at Corinth, and is dealt with in 1 Cor. 8:4-13. It is to be noticed that no rigid commandment is given in regard to this matter, but that considerable latitude is allowed. The chief thing to be considered is the conscience of brethren who are "weak," and who would be stumbled to see another, who is of more robust faith, and has no "conscience of the idol," eating that which had been offered as a sacrifice in an idol temple. The eating or not eating is in itself a matter of no moment, for "meat commendeth us not to God; for neither if we eat are we better; neither if we eat not are we worse" (1 Cor. 8:8). But it *is* a matter of *much* moment that the one who is strong in faith, and can realize that an idol is nothing in the world, should not so use his liberty as to put a stumbling-block in the way of the weak brother. Therefore, the Apostle says, "if meat make my brother to offend (stumble) I will eat no flesh while the world standeth, lest I make my brother to offend" (1 Cor. 8:13).

In Romans 14 no mention is made of things offered to idols. Nevertheless the relation to the passage in 1 Corinthians is obvious, and the latter throws light upon the former.

"Him that is weak in the faith receive ye, but not to doubtful disputations,"—not to reasonings about such matters as whether such and such things should or should not be eaten or drunk. One man believes to eat all things.

Another being weak (in faith) eateth herbs. Very well. Let not such a difference be made an occasion of argument, nor a cause for either *despising* or *judging* one another.

As to the eating or not eating there is no commandment of the Lord. But there *is* a commandment in regard to despising another and judging another. Special prominence is given to the matter of *judging*. "Who art thou that judgest another man's servant? To his own master he standeth or falleth. Yea, he shall (if unable to stand himself) *be holden up;* for God is able to make him *stand*" (verse 4).

"But why dost thou judge thy brother? or why dost thou set at nought (*despise*, same word as in verse 3) thy brother? for we shall *all stand before the judgment seat of Christ*" (verse 10). And *there* every matter will be rightly judged.

"So then every one of us shall give account of himself to God. Let us not therefore judge one another any more. But judge this rather, that no man put a stumbling block, or an occasion to fall in his brother's way" (verses 12, 13).

Nothing is unclean of itself. Defilement does not result from partaking of any particular sort of food. "Not that which goeth into the mouth defileth a man" (Matt. 15:11). Nevertheless "to him that *esteemeth* anything to be unclean, to *him* it *is* unclean" (Rom. 14:14).

The same principle applies to different views as to estimating particular days. "One man esteemeth one day above another." Consequently he may refrain from doing things on that day which he would feel free to do on other days. "Another esteemeth every day alike" (verse 5). Again there is no command as to esteeming or not esteeming one day above another. The kingdom of God is not a matter of eating and drinking (verse 17); neither is it a matter of regarding one day as above another. All that is enjoined in this connection is that "every man be fully persuaded in his own mind."

These are matters between the individual and the Lord. "He that regardeth the day, regardeth it unto the Lord; and he that regardeth not the day, to the Lord he doth not regard it." That is to say, whatever we do in this connection should be as "unto the Lord."

Likewise in the matter of eating or not eating. "He that eateth, eateth to the Lord, for he giveth God thanks; and he that eateth not, to the Lord he eateth not, and giveth God thanks."

We have no right to interfere in that which is between the conscience of a fellow-saint and the Lord; and these are matters which are expressly left to the individual conscience.

This Scripture cannot be properly regarded as giving the slightest countenance to the practice of observing special days as "holy days." The observance of special "days and months, and times, and years" is foreign to Christianity. To indulge in such observance is to turn again unto "bondage" to "the weak and beggarly elements of the world" (Gal. 4:9, 10). The observance of special days and the restriction of diet to certain kinds of foods, belonged to the era of "shadows" which passed away when Christ came (Col. 2:16, 17).

Indeed the passage in Rom. 14 is very far from approving of days to be set apart by ecclesiastical authority and to be observed in some special manner. Had that been its purpose, the holy days which the church was to observe, and the manner of their due observance would surely have been specified with as much particularity as the "Feasts of Jehovah" were specified in Lev. 23. Moreover, in that case it would not be right for any Christian to "esteem every day alike."

In Romans it is an *individual* matter, not a *collective* matter. It is, moreover, a matter of *esteeming* a day, not of prescribing for it certain religious ceremonies. And finally it leaves the saints free to regard all days alike. There could be no such liberty if God had marked any particular days as "holy" during this age, and to be observed by the church. We do not take this Scripture as discountenancing the universal custom among Christians of setting apart the first day of the week as a day of rest from secular occupations, and a day for meeting together for worship, for the ministry of the Word of God, and especially for remembering the Lord in the breaking of bread. The principle of a weekly rest-day existed from the beginning. It was observed by the Israelites before the law of Sinai was given, for God withheld the manna on the seventh day (Ex. 16:22–30). In the primitive church the disciples came together on the first day of the week to break bread (Acts 20:7). It would be a violation of the teaching of Romans 14 to disregard and secularize the first day of the week, as by so doing the majority of Christians would be stumbled or offended. But the numerous feast-days and holy days of Christendom have, for the most part, a pagan origin, and Christians should not take part in their observance. This applies particularly to " Christmas," which is simply a pagan festival in honor of the Sun-

god, and which the world celebrates with heathen and
godless festivities.

It follows that the devising of a system of special days
and seasons is purely a human contrivance, in the nature
of "will worship" (Col. 2:23); and the imposition of such
a system upon the church is the placing of a grievous
man-made yoke upon the necks of the disciples.

"For none of us liveth to himself, and no man
dieth to himself" (Ver. 7).

Here is a fact of very great importance. No matter
how much we may try to live to ourselves we cannot
do it. "Whether we live, we live *unto the Lord*." Every
act of our lives, what we do and what we refrain from
doing, what we eat and what we do not eat, whether
we esteem a day or do not,—everything affects the Lord.
Nothing is overlooked by Him. Nothing is unimportant
to Him. The very hairs of our head are numbered.
Each hair exists in God's sight. *All things* are naked
and open to the eyes of Him with Whom we have
to do.

Moreover, no man dieth to himself. When one dies,
he dies *to the Lord*. "For to this end Christ both died
and rose, and lived again, that He might be LORD both
of the dead and living. . . . For it is written: "As I
live, saith the Lord, every one shall bow to Me, and every
tongue shall confess to God" (Ver. 8–11).

The prominent thought here is the *Lordship* of Jesus
Christ; that is to say, His supreme authority. It is God's
intention that the Lordship of Christ shall be owned in
every part of the universe, "in heaven and in earth, and
under the earth" (Phil. 2:10, 11). It would seem from
Rom. 14:9 that Christ passed, as a Man, through all
these regions, earth, under the earth, and heaven, in

order that He might be " Lord both of the dead and of the living."

"For the kingdom of God is not meat and drink (lit. not eating and drinking) but righteousness, peace, and joy in the Holy Ghost" (Ver. 17).

The connection in which this well-known verse appears indicates its primary significance to be that the kingdom of God, into which believers have been " translated " (Col. 1:13), has not to do with matters of diet —eating and drinking—but with " righteousness, peace, and joy in the Holy Ghost."

Whatever concern we may have about eating and drinking, and whatever attention we may pay to such matters, are of no avail. Our primary concern, as being under the Lordship of Jesus Christ, should be *righteousness*. Under that heading come all the many admonitions in the immediate context, and in other Scriptures, relating to our dealings with our fellow-men, whether converted or unconverted. The same *grace of God* which brought salvation to us also teaches us (lit. *disciplines* us) to the end that we should live *righteously* in this present age (Titus 2:11, 12).

Next, our concern should be to maintain *peace*. Our God is " the God of peace" (15:33). Moreover, verse 19 says: "Let us, therefore, follow after the *things which make for peace*, and things wherewith one may *edify another*." This is in contrast with following after matters of eating and drinking, or regarding special days, which make for strife, instead of peace, and which cause stumbling instead of building up.

To the same effect the Apostle Peter admonishes us to eschew evil, and do good; to seek peace and pursue it (1 Pet. 3:11).

Finally, the kingdom of God, as it now exists during the period of "the mystery" (Mark 4:11); that is to say, while it exists as a kingdom without a present visible King, without the enforcement of His authority, and with His enemies in possession of the earth which is the proper domain of the kingdom, is "joy in the Holy Ghost." This is a joy that can be known only by those who truly acknowledge the Lordship of the absent and rejected King. To them has been given a revelation concerning their relationship with the Father and with the Lord Jesus Christ, and concerning the rapidly approaching " day of the Lord," which should fill their hearts with uninterrupted joy. All of them should share that joy. But occupation with disputes over matters of meat and drink, and of sabbaths, and holy days, quenches it. Let us then give earnest heed to these things, and examine ourselves before the Lord with respect to them.

The closing verses of Rom. 14 (ver. 20-23) refer again to the matter of eating and drinking; showing that this subject extends to the end of the chapter. The words "Hast thou faith? Have it to thyself before God," evidently refer back to verses 1 and 2. The "faith" here is that which enables one to eat of every sort of food with a clear conscience, as distinguished from one who is "weak in the faith," and in consequence fears to eat flesh, but confines himself to herbs. Happy is the man who does not condemn himself in what he allows himself to do; but a man does condemn himself if he does a thing (as eating a particular food) doubtingly. For in such case he is not acting out of faith (or according to faith); and whatever is not out of faith is sin.

CHAPTER XVI.

The God of Patience and Comfort, of Hope and Peace; The Ministry of Jesus Christ, and that of His Servant Paul.

(Rom. 15 and 16.)

The first verse of Rom. 15 continues the subject of the preceding chapter. "We then that are strong (in the faith) ought to bear the infirmities of the weak (in the faith) and not to please ourselves" (in the way we use the liberty which we have in Christ). Here then is something we "ought" (*owe it* to others) to do, namely, to please others unto good, for building them up. Consequently this exhortation comes under the head of Rom. 13:8: "*Owe* (same word as in 15:1) no man anything." This being something we "owe," we are bound to dis-charge the debt.

"For even Christ pleased not Himself." He was ever considerate of others in all that He did while among men, never considering Himself at all. Thus the Scripture keeps the perfect Pattern constantly before our eyes. He bore even the reproaches of others. Ps. 69:9 is here quoted, "The reproaches of them that reproached Thee are fallen upon Me." This is part of a remarkable passage in which the Spirit of Christ in the Prophet David testifies beforehand the sufferings of Christ. Part of those sufferings was to endure reproach. "Because for Thy sake I have borne reproach." "Thou hast known My reproach, and My shame, and My dishonour" (Ps. 69:7, 19). "A reproach of men and despised of the people" (Ps. 22:6). "Reproach hath broken my heart" (Ps. 69:20). This is the " endurance of the Christ" into which the Apostle prays our hearts may be directed. (2 Thess. 3:5 Gr.).

These things, which were written aforetime, were written for our instruction, that we, through *endurance*, and encouragement of the Scriptures might have *hope*.

"For whatsoever things were written aforetime were written for our learning, that we through patience, and the comfort of the Scriptures, might have hope" (ver. 4).

There are two factors mentioned here as contributing to the production of hope. *First*, patience or endurance, as is written in Chap. 5:4, "patience (worketh) experience, and experience hope." But the patience enjoined in Chap. 15 appears to be not endurance under tribulation, but rather patience in bearing the infirmities of "weak" brethren.

The second factor is the "comfort," or encouragement, or the strengthening influence, of the Scriptures. The Scriptures are the resource of the saints for strength or encouragement, or "comfort," in time of trial or difficulty, or pressure of any kind. There are promises, almost without number, upon which we may lay firm hold when difficulties and adversities press upon us.

Then, in the next verse, the God Who gave us the Scriptures is very beautifully called "the God of patience and comfort,"—the two things named in verse 4. This expression binds the verse very closely to verse 4; but unhappily the closeness of the connection is obscured by the substitution of the word "consolation" for "comfort"; whereas, in both verses the words in the original Greek are identical, "patience and comfort," or "endurance and encouragement." So the force of the Scripture is this: God desires that we should have "hope"; and the need of it has been already pointed out. Hope is to be had through patience, and the comfort of the Scriptures. And God (Who having spared not His own Son cannot withhold anything from us) is Himself the God of patience and comfort. To Him, therefore, the Apostle prays that He would grant to the saints to be likeminded one toward another; that is to say, likeminded as was Christ Who pleased not Himself: That they might with *one mind* and one mouth glorify God, even the Father of our Lord Jesus Christ (ver. 6).

This oneness of the saints is that which God greatly desires to see. To whatever extent it exists He is glorified. To whatever extent divisions and discords exist, instead of oneness of mind, He is dishonoured. Here is something to give to every saint of God occasion for deep exercise of heart, for self-examination to see if there be possible causes of division in himself, and for continual prayer and intercession.

"Wherefore," *i. e.* with a view to the unity whereby God is glorified, "receive ye one another, as Christ also received us *to the glory of God*." (Ver. 7.)

Here it is plainly stated that we should receive one another as Christ has received us, and that our doing this is to the glory of God. Christ has received us with all our manifold imperfections and failures, and with manifold erroneous views as to the truth; and He knows them *all.* The Scripture says that when we *receive* a fellow-saint, though he be " weak," and though we may see in him much that we disapprove, we do thereby *glorify God*. It is never said that God is glorified when saints *reject* others. Yet how often that is done for the avowed reason that it is for the glory or honour of the Lord! Surely the " weak " ones have a special claim upon such as are " strong." By receiving them they can be helped. By rejecting them they can only be harmed.

One of the reproaches that Christ bore was that He *received* sinners. "This man *receiveth* sinners, and eateth with them" (Luke 15:2). So ought we to receive one another as Christ has received us.

The Ministry of Jesus Christ.

The mention of the fact that Christ received us in our sinfulness, ignorance, and wretchedness, introduces the subject of the ministry of the Lord Jesus towards Jews and Gentiles. Accordingly, at this point the Apostle states that Jesus Christ became a Servant ("minister") of the circumcision, on behalf of the truth of God, for to confirm the promises made to the fathers. All the promises of God made of old time to the fathers in Israel, were dependent for their fulfilment upon Christ. So He became a Servant of the circumcision to fulfil those promises, in order that not one part of the " truth of God " should fail. Grace and *truth* came by Jesus Christ. But more than that. He came also in order " that *the Gentiles* might glorify God for His mercy; as it is written: For this cause I will confess to Thee among the Gentiles (quoting Ps. 18:49). "And again He saith, Rejoice ye Gentiles *with His people* " (quoting Deut. 32:43).

Thus we see that the ministry of Jesus Christ had for its complete object the bringing of Jews and Gentiles together into one body, as set forth in the preceding chapters. Or, as stated in Ephesians 2:14-16: He hath made both Jew and Gentile to be one in Himself, having broken down the partition wall that had previously kept them apart, " for to make in Himself of twain (Jew and Gentile) one new man, making peace, and that He might reconcile both unto God in one body by the cross, having slain the enmity thereby."

Other Scriptures which Jesus Christ fulfilled through His earthly ministry are also quoted: "And again, Praise the Lord, all ye Gentiles; and laud Him all ye people " (Ps. 117:1). In this and similar passages the " people " means Israel. " And again, Esaias saith, There shall be a root of Jesse, and He that shall rise to *reign* over the Gentiles. *In Him shall the Gentiles have hope* " (Quoting Is. 11:1 and 10).

It is important to note that the word here is "hope," not "trust," as in the A. V. For the hope which the Gentiles have in the Christ of God, Who was the special hope of Israel, is the prominent feature of the gospel committed to Paul. This Scripture connects with the opening words of the Epistle, "the gospel of God, concerning His Son, Who was made *of the seed of David* according to flesh." Jesus Christ is this Son of David, the Branch out of the root of Jesse, " Which shall stand for an ensign of the people (Israel) and to it shall the Gentiles seek. *And His rest shall be glorious*" (Is. 11:10).

Moreover, the word "hope" at the end of Rom. 15:12 leads into the very beautiful and consoling words of verse 13: "Now the God of *hope*, fill you with all joy and peace *in believing*, that ye may *abound in hope*, through the power of the Holy Ghost." God is the "God of Hope" for the Gentile as well as for the Jew.

Peace and joy in the Holy Ghost are characteristic of the Kingdom of God (14:17). The God of hope fills us with these, as we "believe" the revelations of His mercy and grace here given to us. May we indeed "abound in hope," that the purpose of the ministry of the Son of God, and of the Sacrifice which He offered on our behalf, may be accomplished in us.

The Ministry of the Apostle Paul (ver. 15-21).

Paul now refers to the "grace of God" bestowed upon himself that he should be the minister of Jesus Christ *to the Gentiles*, ministering to them the *Gospel of God*; to the end that the offering up *of the Gentiles* (as typified by one of the wave loaves offered on Pentecost—see the comments in this volume on Rom. 11:16), might be acceptable, being sanctified by the Holy Ghost.

So likewise in Ephesians, after speaking of the ministry of the Lord Jesus in abolishing the middle wall of partition between Jew and Gentile, Paul refers to "the grace of God" which was given him toward the *Gentiles* (Eph. 3:2), and says "Unto me, who am less than the least of all saints is this grace given, that I should preach *among the Gentiles* the unsearchable riches of Christ" (Eph. 3:8.)

Thus it appears that the special service committed to Paul was to carry on that branch of the Lord's own ministry which had reference to the Gentiles. (See also Acts 22:21, and 26:17, 18.) Therefore, Paul had whereof he might boast in those things which pertain to God. For he would not dare to speak of his own doings, but only of the things that *Christ* had wrought through him, by word and deed, to make the Gentiles obedient to the faith, through mighty signs and wonders, by the power of the Spirit of God. (Cf. Heb. 2:3, 4.)

Paul takes no credit to himself for the signs and wonders wrought by him, or for his labours in the Gospel, or for the results achieved thereby. In 1 Cor. 15:10 he states the fact that he laboured in the gospel more abundantly than all the other Apostles; but adds "Yet (it was) not I, but the grace of God which was with me."

So mightily did the power of the Spirit of God work through this frail instrument, that by him the gospel of Christ had been fully preached already from Jerusalem (God's starting point) round about into Illyricum; and in after years it was carried by him much farther. The limits of Paul's preaching are not known with certainty, but this chapter states his purpose to take a journey into Spain (ver. 24).

Considering the great hindrances that were ever in his path, the natural difficulties of the way, and the fierce and unrelenting opposition of the enemies of truth, we may well marvel at what God accomplished through this weak instrument.

In verse 20 Paul tells of his "ambition," saying, "Yea, so have I strived (lit. was *ambitious*) to preach the gospel, not where Christ was named, lest I should build upon another man's foundation; but as it was written: To whom He was not spoken of, they shall see; and they that have not heard shall understand."

This is a quotation from Is. 52:15, showing that Paul's mission was to proclaim among the heathen (that is, the Gentiles who had no promise of Christ, and no hope) the Divine Sufferer of Isaiah 53, Who was to bear the 'iniquities of many, and pour out His soul an offering for sin.

The fulfilment of this great ministry had so occupied the time of the Apostle that he had been unable, up to that date, to come to Rome. "But now having no more place in these parts," that is to say, no more place to preach where Christ was unknown, and having desired for many years to come to Rome, he purposed doing so on his way to Spain.

But Paul had first to fulfil a ministry to the poor saints at Jerusalem, in bringing to them a contribution made by the Gentile believers in Macedonia and Achaia. This mission was fraught with danger from unbelieving Jews, on account of which Paul desired the prayers of the saints at Rome (ver. 31, 32). Moreover, his strong desire was to go to Rome. But he pleased not himself; and so he turned back to Jerusalem to fulfil the service to the "poor saints" there, before pursuing his own desire.

This was in accordance with the agreement reached with the other Apostles, as recorded in Gal. 2:9, 10, where Paul says: "And when James, Cephas and John . . . perceived the *grace that was given to me* (that is to preach Christ among the Gentiles) they gave to me and Barnabas the right hands of fellowship; that we should go unto the heathen (Gentiles) and they unto the circumcision. Only they would that we should *remember the poor; the same which I also was forward to do.*"

In the 9th chapter of 2 Cor. Paul again refers to this service to the poor saints, and makes mention of the contributions of the believers in Macedonia and Achaia (ver. 2).

The Apostle makes this incident the occasion for laying down an important principle. He declares that the

Gentile believers are the "debtors" of the Jews. This is a fact that is generally lost sight of. It should therefore be pressed upon the attention of Gentile believers that they are the *debtors* of the Israelites. "For if the Gentiles have been made partakers of *their* (the Israelites') spiritual things, their duty is also to minister unto them in carnal things" (ver. 27).

We have already commented at some length upon the marvelous "spiritual things" which originally pertained to the Israelites, but in which we Gentiles have been made partakers by grace, through the Gospel. Therefore, we need only notice, at this point, that, in consequence of our participation in their spiritual things, it becomes our "duty" to minister unto them in carnal things. Let us see to the discharge of this duty.

The Apostle is sure that he will come to the Roman saints in the fulness of the blessing of the Gospel of Christ (ver. 29). That *good-news concerning the Christ*, which Paul announced among the Gentiles, according to the revelation of the mystery, embraces in its grand scope every spiritual blessing wherewith God has blessed us in the heavenly places in Christ (Eph. 1:3). Such is "the fulness of the blessing of the gospel of Christ."

Chapter 16 of Romans is occupied mainly with personal greetings, and offers little occasion for comment. Although Paul had never been to Rome he was personally known to a number of the saints there. Among these were Priscilla and Aquila (ver. 3), Jews who had been previously banished from Rome with all other Jews by a decree of Claudius Caeser (Acts 18:1-3), and whom Paul had met at Corinth; but who had since returned again to Rome. Paul refers to them as having laid down their own necks for his life. Moreover, he says, "Unto whom not only I give thanks, but also *all the churches of the Gentiles.*" At Rome there was a church in their house (ver. 5).

In marked contrast to these loving salutations is the warning of verses 17, 18. "Now I beseech you, brethren, mark them which cause divisions and offences (*skandala*) contrary to the doctrine which ye have learned; and avoid them. For they that are such serve not our Lord Jesus Christ, but their own belly; and by good words and fair-speaking (by kind speaking and praise) deceive the hearts of the simple."

Those who serve the Lord Jesus Christ labour, as Paul did, striving with great conflict, that the saints might be *united in one body*, their hearts being knit together in love. On the contrary, it is a grievous offense to the Lord, and an injury to His members, to cause divisions. They who do so, notwithstanding their fair speech and flattering words, are not the servants of the Lord, but serve their own personal ends. The "doctrine" which the saints "have learned" is to receive one another and cherish one another, with long suffering, forbearing one another, in love endeavoring to keep the unity of the spirit, to be kindly affectioned one to another with brotherly love. In a word, right doctrine draws the saints together. Separations are contrary to the doctrine of Christ.

The saints themselves are responsible to keep their eye on such mischief-makers; and to turn away from them, not following their leadership.

God would have us to be "wise unto that which is good, and simple concerning evil" (ver. 19). It is, of course, needful that we should recognize the evil condition of things around us. But on the other hand there is a sense in which it may be said that the less we know about evil the better. For it is very easy to become occupied with the dark side of things, to take a gloomy satisfaction in contemplating the depravity and corruption of human nature, and to imagine ourselves to be better than others because we comment with severity on the wrong-doings of society in general. There are many observers of present social, industrial and political conditions who are thoroughly acquainted with the corruption that abounds everywhere, and who make it their constant theme. But their accurate knowledge of the existing evils results in no benefit to themselves or to others.

It is far better to be occupied with that which is good. As in 12:21, "Be not overcome of evil, but overcome evil with good." All things, however evil their nature, work together *for good* to them that love God. So let our minds dwell on the things of God, His grace, His goodness, His righteousness, His wisdom, and His love. The good will eventually triumph, and even the evil, so long as it lasts, is compelled, by the overruling power of God, to serve His purposes.

"And," continues the Apostle, "the God of peace shall bruise Satan (the author of evil) under your feet *shortly*" (ver. 20). Again we have the heartening assurance that the time of the seeming supremacy of evil is *short*. The God of peace, Who knows the future as well as the past, gives us this assurance. The hour of the bruising of Satan, which will be the fulfilment of the earliest prophecy (Gen. 3:15), is near.

The titles of God in these chapters should be noticed, for they are full of encouragement for those who are yet in the place of trial. He is "the God of patience and comfort" (15:5), "the God of hope" (15:13), "the God of peace" (15:33 and 16:20), and "the God only wise" (16:27). And all that He has and is "for us," His children.

Such is the "Gospel of God concerning His Son Jesus Christ our Lord," as committed to His servant Paul, and through him made known to us, in accordance with the revelation of the mystery which was kept secret since the world began, but now is made known to all nations for the obedience of faith. It is a wondrous revelation, containing breadths and lengths and depths and heights of love, and wisdom and power, and unsearchable riches of grace and glory. It is manifestly Divine; for such a message never did or could originate in the mind of men. Therefore it demands the faith and obedience of all men, and it imparts the full assurance of hope to all who believe.

Therefore, "to God only wise, be glory through Jesus Christ forever. Amen."

www.ingramcontent.com/pod-product-compliance
Lightning Source LLC
Chambersburg PA
CBHW070449090426
42735CB00012B/2498